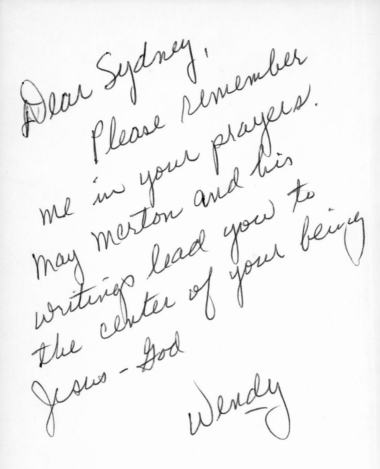

Dear Sydney,

Please remember me in your prayers. May Merton and his writings lead you to the center of your being Jesus - God

Wendy

SPIRITUAL DIRECTION AND MEDITATION

BY

THOMAS MERTON

THE LITURGICAL PRESS

Nihil obstat ex parte Ordinis: Fr. M. Thomas Aquinas Porter; Fr. M. Paul Bourne; Fr. M. Shane Regan. *Imprimi potest*: Fr. M. Gabriel Sortais, Abbot General. January 16, 1960.

Nihil obstat: John Eidenschink, O.S.B., J.C.D., *Censor deputatus*. *Imprimatur*: ✠ Peter W. Bartholome, D.D., Bishop of St. Cloud. December 14, 1959.

PREFACE

This booklet contains a revised and considerably expanded version of material on spiritual direction and meditation which appeared, in installments, in the magazine *Sponsa Regis*. The first part is addressed to the Christian, particularly to the religious, who seeks a director or who has one, and who desires to take full advantage of his opportunities. At the same time, it is hoped that some priests who are too shy to regard themselves as potential "spiritual directors" may, by reading these pages, learn to overcome their natural hesitations and, relying on the help of God, be emboldened to give advice and encouragement in the confessional when there is time to do so.

At the same time it is hoped that some over-rigid and stereotyped ideas about direction may be partially dispelled by one of the points made in these pages, namely, that the director is not to be regarded as a magical machine for solving cases and declaring the holy will of God beyond all hope of appeal, but a trusted friend who, in an atmosphere of sympathetic understanding, helps and strengthens us in our groping efforts to correspond with the grace of the Holy Spirit, who alone is the true Director in the fullest sense of the word.

It is also emphasized that, since grace builds on nature, we can best profit by spiritual direction if we are encouraged to develop our natural simplicity, sincerity, and forthright spiritual honesty, in a word to "be ourselves" in the best sense of the expression. In this way, a healthy and widespread use of this important means to perfection will help Christians to keep in vital contact with the reality of their vocation and of their life, instead of losing themselves in a maze of abstract devotional fictions.

The second part of the book is made up of notes on meditation which were written in 1951 as a kind of companion to *What is Contemplation?* After they had been typed out, they were laid aside and forgotten. They are now being printed with additions and corrections. You cannot learn meditation from a book. You just have to *meditate*. However, we can all agree that a few hints at the right time and in the right words may make a great deal of difference.

We hope that these few pages may help someone who has not been able to find what he needed in the other books on the subject. That is sufficient reason for their publication, assuming that there is nothing radically wrong with our approach. There should not be. It is perfectly traditional and familiar. The only striking characteristic of this approach is its informality and its aversion to conventional and rigid systems. Not that there is anything wrong with systems of meditation —

and certainly an aversion to systems must not be interpreted as a repugnance for discipline. Discipline is most important, and without it no serious meditation will ever be possible. But it should be *one's own* discipline, not a routine mechanically imposed from the outside.

Here, then, are these pages which do not pretend to be complete, thorough or exhaustive. They simply touch on a few of the important points that anyone needs to understand before he can really meditate well. Nowhere in these notes have I insisted that meditation is important, and nowhere have I tried to sell anyone the idea of meditating. That is because all this is taken for granted. This book is not for people who do not want to meditate. It is only for those who are already interested, and who would like to meditate every day.

The factor of *desire* is, of course, extremely important. One of the main reasons why people who take up meditation fail to get anywhere in it is that they go about it halfheartedly, without any serious interest. It should be taken as obvious that a man who has no real desire to meditate will certainly not succeed; for here is one place, before all others, where you have to do the job yourself, aided by the grace of God. Nobody else is going to do it for you.

Abbey of Gethsemani
Fall, 1959

SPIRITUAL DIRECTION
AND MEDITATION

SPIRITUAL DIRECTION

1. *The Meaning and Purpose of Spiritual Direction*

The original, primitive meaning of spiritual direction suggests a particular need connected with a special ascetic task, a peculiar vocation for which a professional formation is required. In other words, spiritual direction is a monastic concept. It is a practice which was unnecessary until men withdrew from the Christian community in order to live as solitaries in the desert. For the ordinary member of the primitive Christian community there was no particular need of personal direction in the professional sense. The bishop, the living and visible representative of the apostle who had founded the local Church, spoke for Christ and the apostles, and, helped by the presbyters, took care of all the spiritual needs of his flock. The individual member of the community was "formed" and "guided" by his participation in the life of the community, and such instruction as was needed was given first of all by the bishop and presbyters, and then, through informal admonitions, by one's parents, spouse, friends and fellow Christians.

But when the first solitaries retired to the desert, they

3

separated themselves from the Christian community. Their departure into the wilderness was approved and, in a sense, canonized by no less a bishop than St. Athanasius, soon followed by many others. But they lived solitary and dangerous lives, far from any church, and rarely participating even in the Mystery of the Eucharist. Yet they had gone into the wilderness to seek Christ. They had, like Christ, been "led by the Spirit into the wilderness to be tempted." And, like the Lord Himself, they were to be tempted by the evil one. Hence the need for "discernment of spirits" — and for a director.

We look back after many centuries upon the desert fathers and interpret their vocation in the light of our own. After all, they were the "first religious." We do not see how very different, in many ways, were their lives from ours. In any event, their deliberate withdrawal from the normal life of the visible Church was a very perilous spiritual adventure and an innovation of a type that would undoubtedly be considered out of the question by many today. In this adventure, certain safeguards were absolutely essential, and the most obvious and important of these was the training and guidance of the novice by a "spiritual father." In this case, the spiritual father replaced the bishop and presbyter as representative of Christ. And yet there was a difference because there was nothing hierarchical about his function. It was purely and simply charismatic. It was sanctioned by the father's own personal holiness. The greatest "abbots" in the Egyptian and Syrian deserts were generally not priests.

The *Apothegmata* or "Sayings of the Fathers" remain as an eloquent witness to the simplicity and depth of this spiritual guidance. Disciples travelled often for miles through the wilderness just to hear a brief word of advice, a "word of salvation" which summed up the judgment and the will of God for them in their actual, concrete situation. The impact of these "words" resided not so much in their simple content as in the inward action of the Holy Spirit which accompanied them, in the soul of the hearer. This of course presupposes an ardent faith, and a deep hunger for the word of God and for salvation. This spiritual appetite, this need for light, had in its turn been generated by tribulation and compunction. "Direction" then was God's answer to a need created in the soul by trial and compunction, and communicated through a charismatic representative of the Mystical Body, the *Abbas*, or spiritual Father.

This brings us to the root meaning of spiritual direction. It is a continuous process of formation and guidance, in which a Christian is led and encouraged *in his special vocation*, so that by faithful correspondence to the graces of the Holy Spirit he may attain to the particular end of his vocation and to union with God. This union with God signifies not only the vision of God in heaven but, as Cassian specifies, that perfect purity of heart which, even on earth, constitutes sanctity and attains to an obscure experience of heavenly things. Spiritual direction was, then, one of the essential means to monastic perfection.

This description of spiritual direction brings out certain important differences between direction and counselling, or direction and psychotherapy. Spiritual direction is not merely the cumulative effect of encouragements and admonitions which we all need in order to live up to our state in life. It is not mere ethical, social or psychological guidance. It is *spiritual*.

But it is important for us to understand what this word "spiritual" means here. There is a temptation to think that spiritual direction is the guidance of one's spiritual activities, considered as a small part or department of one's life. You go to a spiritual director to have him take care of your spirit, the way you go to a dentist to have him take care of your teeth, or to a barber to get a haircut. This is completely false. The spiritual director is concerned with the *whole person*, for the spiritual life is not just the life of the mind, or of the affections, or of the "summit of the soul" — it is the life of the whole person. For the spiritual man (*pneumatikos*) is one whose whole life, in all its aspects and all its activities, has been spiritualized by the action of the Holy Spirit, whether through the sacraments or by personal and interior inspirations. Moreover, spiritual direction is concerned with the whole person not simply as an individual human being, but as a son of God, another Christ, seeking to recover the perfect likeness to God in Christ, and by the Spirit of Christ.

The spiritual man is one who, "whether he eats or drinks or whatever else he does, does all for the glory of God" (1 Cor. 10:31). Again, this does not mean that he merely registers in his mind an abstract intention to glorify God. It means that in all his actions he is free from the superficial automatism of conventional routine. It means that in all that he does he acts freely, simply, spontaneously, from the depths of his heart, moved by love.

Originally, as we have said, the concept of the "spiritual father" is linked up with the idea of a special vocation, and very particular risks. But of course, all through the history of monasticism, we see evidence that the monk tends to become, in certain cases, the spiritual father to all comers, and to give advice about everything. This was quite common for example among the Cistercian laybrothers in 12th century England, some of whom acquired a great reputation for their ability to read and guide souls. Perhaps there was some element of nonsense in this sudden popular craze: the same kind of credulity that led people to frequent the recluses and anchoresses immured near village churches, who, though doubtless quite pious, had a universal reputation for being gossips. Nevertheless, we must not judge these manifestations of popular piety too harshly.

There is no doubt that the Lord has, in the past, reached souls very effectively in this way, and we must not make the mistake of thinking that direction is a luxury reserved for a special elite. For if, as Eric Gill said, "every man is a special kind of artist" it is perhaps true that every man has a special and even perilous vocation to complete the supreme work of art which is his sanctification. Hence the apt saying of a Russian *Staretz* who was criticized for spending time seriously advising an old peasant woman about the care of her turkeys. "Not at all," he replied, "her *whole life* is in those turkeys." Direction, then, speaks to the whole man, in the concrete circumstances of his life, however simple they may be. It is not a question of discussing the relative merits of the discipline and the hairshirt, and determining whether or not one has reached the "prayer of quiet."

The whole purpose of spiritual direction is to penetrate beneath the surface of a man's life, to get behind the façade of conventional gestures and attitudes which he presents to the world, and to bring out his inner spiritual freedom, his inmost truth, which is what we call the likeness of Christ in his soul. This is entirely a supernatural thing, for the work of rescuing the inner man from automatism belongs first of all to the Holy Spirit. The spiritual director cannot do such a work himself. His function is to verify and to encourage what is truly spiritual in the soul. He must teach others to "discern" between good and evil tendencies, to distinguish the inspirations of the spirit of evil from those of the Holy Spirit. A spiritual director is, then, one who helps another to recognize and to follow the inspirations of grace in his life, in order to arrive at the end to which God is leading him. And this, as we have said, originally presupposed a special vocation. A spiritual director was necessary, above all, for one who had been called to seek God by an unusual and perilous road. It must not be forgotten that the spiritual director in primitive times was much more than the present name implies. He was a spiritual father who "begot" the perfect life in the soul of his disciple by his instructions first of all, but also by his prayer, his sanctity and his example. He was to the young monk a kind of "sacrament" of the Lord's presence in the ecclesiastical community.

In the earliest days of Christian monasticism the spiritual father did much more than instruct and advise. The neophyte lived in the same cell with him, day and night, and did what he saw his father doing. He made known to the father "all the thoughts that came into his heart" and was told, on the spot, how to react. In this way he learned the whole spiritual life in a concrete and experimental way. He literally absorbed and reproduced in his own life the life and spirit of his "father in Christ."

The same concept of spiritual fatherhood persists today in Asia, for example in Yoga, where the difficult and complex disciplines can only be properly learned from a *guru* who is considered not only an expert in his professional field, but a representative and instrument of God. Russian literature of the nineteenth century introduces us to the figures of remarkable spiritual directors, *startzi*, holy monks who exercised a great influence in the life of the time, not only on the poor and humble, as we have just seen, but also on the intelligentsia.

It is important that we recover the full idea of spiritual direction and rescue the concept from its impoverished condition — according to which the director is merely one to whom we apply for quasi-infallible solutions to moral and ascetic "cases." If this is what we mean by a director, we will find that our understanding will be perverted by a kind of magic and pragmatic conventionalism. The "director" is thought to be one endowed with special, almost miraculous, authority and has the power to give the "right formula" when it is asked for. He is treated as a machine for producing answers that will work, that will clear up difficulties and make us perfect. He has a "system," or rather, he has become an expert in the workings of somebody else's system — which, having been approved by the Church, is devoutly believed to be infallible in every case, no matter how it is applied, and even if it is used arbitrarily with supreme disregard for individual circumstances. Such spiritual direction is mechanical, and it tends to frustrate the real purpose of genuine spiritual guidance.

It tends to reinforce the mechanisms and routines with which the soul is destroying its own capacity for a spontaneous response to grace.

The first thing that genuine spiritual direction requires in order to work properly is a normal, spontaneous human relationship. We must not suppose that it is somehow "not supernatural" to open ourselves easily to a director and converse with him in an atmosphere of pleasant and easy familiarity. This aids the work of grace : another example of grace building on nature.

It is a paradox that those who are the most rigidly "supernatural" in their theory of the spiritual life are sometimes the most "natural" in practice. To imagine that faith can only operate in a situation that is humanly repugnant, and that the "supernatural" decisions are only those which the penitent finds revolting or practically impossible, is to frustrate the whole purpose of direction. Some directors, under pretext of acting entirely according to "supernatural principles," are tyrannical and arbitrary. They allow themselves to ignore or overlook the individual needs and weaknesses of their penitents. They have standard answers which are "hard sayings" that admit of no exception and no mitigation and are always the same, no matter how the case may be altered by circumstances. Thus they take satisfaction in secretly indulging their aggressive instincts.

Obviously, we must be prepared to be told things we do not like and we must meet demands that are supremely exacting. We must be ready for sacrifice. And a good director will not hesitate to impose a sacrifice when he believes that it is the will of God. But the trouble is that a certain type of spirituality is arbitrary and unfeeling as a matter of deliberate policy. It assumes as a basic axiom of the spiritual life that every soul needs to be humiliated, frustrated and beaten down; that all spontaneous aspirations are suspect by the very fact that they are spontaneous; that everything individual is to be cut away, and that the soul is to be reduced to a state of absolute, machine-like conformity with others in the same fantastic predicament. Result: a procession of robot "victim souls" moving jerkily from exercise to exercise in the spiritual life, secretly hating the whole business and praying for an early death, meanwhile "offering it up" so that the whole may not be lost.

Obviously, no direction at all is preferable to such direction as this. It is the bane of the religious life.

The seventeenth-century Benedictine mystic, Dom Augustine Baker, who fought a determined battle for the interior liberty of contemplative souls in an age ridden by autocratic directors, has the following to say on the subject: "The director is not to teach his own way, nor indeed any determinate way of prayer, but to instruct his disciples how they may themselves find out the way proper for them. . . . In a word, he is only God's usher, and must lead souls in God's way, and not his own."

2. Is Direction Necessary?

The answer to this question has been prepared by the opening paragraphs of our study. Strictly speaking, spiritual direction is not necessary for the ordinary Christian. But wherever there is *a special mission or vocation* a certain minimum of direction is implied by the very nature of the vocation itself. Let us clarify.

First, let us briefly consider the place of direction in the life of the ordinary Christian layman. Strictly speaking, the ordinary contacts of the faithful with their pastor and confessor are sufficient to take care of their needs. But, of course, this implies that they are known to their pastor and that they have a regular confessor. In a very large parish, where contacts with the pastor may perhaps be at a minimum or even non-existent, then certainly one should at least have a regular confessor to whom he is known, even though the confessor may not be formally and explicitly a "spiritual director." The reason for this is that confession itself implies a certain minimum of spiritual direction. The confessor is bound to instruct and direct the penitent at least to the extent that this is necessary for a fruitful reception of the sacrament of penance. But where one is habitually sinning gravely, advice and special instructions are certainly necessary if the penitent is to take effective steps to avoid sin. And if he is not prepared to take such steps, can it be said that he is fruitfully receiving the sacrament ? Hence, even ordinary confession should involve *some spiritual direction*. It is very unfortunate that many busy priests have come to forget or to neglect this obligation; but perhaps in some cases it is morally impossible to fulfill.

However, this kind of "direction" which is inseparable from the sacrament of penance is not really what we mean by spiritual direction in the present study. It does not go deep enough, and it does not aim at the orientation of one's whole life, with a special ascetic vocation or apostolic mission in view.

One might suppose that because the layman is not in a "state of perfection" he does not need this kind of direction. But certainly, wherever a layman has a special work to do for the Church, or is in a situation with peculiar problems, he certainly ought to have a director. For instance, workers in Catholic action, college students, professional men, or couples preparing for matrimony need some spiritual direction.

So much for the layman. For the religious, direction is a much more serious matter. It would seem that spiritual direction is morally necessary for a religious. Anyone who freely adopts certain professional means for attaining to union with God naturally needs to receive a special formation. He or she needs to be taught the meaning of his vocation, its spirit, its aims and its characteristic problems.

This means something much deeper than a mere exterior formation — learning how to keep the rules, how to carry out the various rites and observances of community life. From the moment one enters into a strictly institutionalized life, in which everything is regulated down to the minutest detail, intimate personal direction becomes a morally necessary *safeguard against deformation*. It is false to imagine that mere external observance of the rules of a religious community is sufficient to educate the novice interiorly and give him the proper spiritual orientation demanded by his new state. Unless, in personal direction, the rules and observances are explained, unless they are applied to the actual circumstances of the life of the individual, they will infallibly produce a spirit of uncomprehending and lifeless routine. Without a really interior and sensitive direction during the crucial period of formation, a young religious is likely to be placed in a very delicate situation, and, indeed, his whole life may be turned into a meaningless pantomime of perfection. Happiness in the religious life really depends on wise direction, especially during the period of formation. Of course, a religious can be "saved" without a good director. That is not the point. The question is, can he lead a fruitful, happy, intelligent spiritual life? Without at least some direction, this is hardly possible. But of course, the direction of a priest, of a theologian, or a specialist is not necessarily indicated here. Where sisters are concerned, a wise prioress or a good novice mistress should be capable of some direction in this sense.

Even after the period of formation the professed religious needs direction. In some cases the more serious problems are not met with until after one has made profession. It is then that direction is most of all necessary, in certain circumstances. It is very important for all newly professed religious to enjoy, if possible, a guidance that is fairly continuous, though not necessarily frequent. What is most to be desired is the intimate direction of someone who knows and understands them, in an atmosphere of informality and trust which perhaps may not be easy to achieve with the superior. Those who have years of experience in the religious life are presumably able to direct themselves — but even they sometimes need to consult a wise spiritual guide. No religious should assume that he has absolutely no need, at any time, of spiritual direction.

It will be noticed that we by no means assume the same need for spiritual direction in all religious. The young need it more than the old, but in fact everything depends on the individual case. In general, however, we might profitably reiterate the statement that a mature religious should normally be able to direct himself. Certainly anyone with a position of responsibility or with a difficult assignment finds that he has to make many decisions for which he alone is accountable in the presence of God. He may even have to solve problems which it is impossible to refer to the judgment of any other human being. This places him in a truly dreadful solitude. Some religious and priests are filled with terror at the very thought of such decisions. And yet that is an error. We should not flee from responsibility, and we should not make such a fetish out of spiritual direction that, even though we are mature and responsible clerics, we refuse to move an inch without being "put under obedience" — in other words without someone else assuming responsibility for us. Needless to say, the concept that we are to "obey" a director in all things is another error, as will be explained later on. The normal religious ought to develop the virtue of prudence, in line with his religious formation, and guide himself when he cannot or need not seek guidance from another. This implies trust in God and a sincere abandonment to the Holy Spirit, from whom we can at any time rely on the light of divine Counsel, provided that we are conscientious religious and try to be men of prayer.

It is not necessary to add that through the course of the ages spiritual direction has become a special function, separate from that of the superior and even from that of the confessor. In early organized monasticism the abbot was at the same time not only the canonical superior of all the monks, but at the same time their spiritual director and confessor. Today the superior is forbidden to hear the confession of his subjects except in certain rare cases. He can, however, be their spiritual director. Very often spiritual direction is separated from confession, and "direction" is given by a specially qualified priest, perhaps on rare occasions. Today most people are lucky if they can find someone who can "give them direction" when they are burdened by accumulated problems. The ideal would be for everyone to have a father to whom he or she could go for regular direction. Superiors will always be ready to grant permission for conscience letters to be sent to a qualified director. The code guarantees access to any confessor with faculties.

However, spiritual directors are not easy to find, even in the religious life. Even where there are several priests at hand, this does not mean that they are all suitable as "directors." The scarcity of really good spiritual directors for religious may perhaps account for the magnitude of the problems in certain communities. Sometimes religious do not receive a really adequate formation, and they are nevertheless professed with unfortunate consequences. After profession, the effects of a good novitiate may vanish into thin air, through lack of a director to continue the work that was well begun. No doubt many losses of vocation could have been prevented by a really solid and firm spiritual direction in the first years after the novitiate.

Those who are firmly grounded and who can share their knowledge and their strength with others receive in this process lights which are of inestimable value for their own religious lives. Nevertheless, even for a superior, a timely conference with a good director may resolve many apparently hopeless problems and open one's eyes to unsuspected dangers, thereby preventing a disaster.

At all times, spiritual direction is of the greatest value to a religious. Even though it may not be strictly necessary, it is always useful. In many cases the absence of direction may mean the difference between sanctity and mediocrity in the religious life. Naturally, one who has sought direction and not found it will not be held responsible for its lack, and God Himself will make up to the soul what is wanting to it in His own way.

We have said above that good directors are rare. This, in fact, is a rather important matter. If we really desire spiritual directors for our communities and for others, let us seek them. We can at least pray for this intention! In the last ten years there has been an amazing growth in the publishing of spiritual books and in the study of the spiritual life. This growth has come at a time when it was needed and desired by the faithful. If it is realized that there is not only a need for spiritual direction, but also a very real hunger for it on the part of religious, directors will soon begin to be more numerous, for God will send them. He will raise up priests who will desire to give themselves to this kind of work, in spite of the difficulties and sacrifices involved. But there is always a danger that the priest qualified to seriously direct religious will be overwhelmed by the demand for his services. His first duty, if he wants to be an effective director, is to see to his own interior life and take time for prayer and meditation, since he will never be able to give to others what he does not possess himself.

3. *How to Profit by Direction*

Setting aside this urgent problem, let us suppose that one has found a director. How can he make the best use of this grace? In the first place, those who have regular spiritual direction ought to realize that this is a gift of God, and even though they may not be thoroughly satisfied, they should humbly appreciate the fact that they have direction at all. This will enable them to take advantage of what they have, and they may perhaps see that supernaturally they are much better off than they realized. Gratitude will make them more attentive to the direction they receive and will attune their faith to possibilities which they had overlooked. Even if their director is not another St. Benedict or St. John of the Cross, they may come to realize that he is nevertheless speaking to them in the name of Christ and acting as His instrument in their lives.

What are we normally entitled to expect from spiritual direction? It is certainly very helpful, but we must not imagine that it works wonders. Some people, and especially some religious who ought to know better, seem to think that they ought to be able to find a spiritual director who with one word can make all their problems vanish. They are not looking for a director but for a miracle-worker. In point of fact, we very often depend on someone else to solve problems that we ought to be able to solve, not so much by our own wisdom as by our generosity in facing the facts and obligations that represent for us the will of God. Nevertheless, human nature is weak, and the kindly support and wise advice of one whom we trust often enables us to *accept* more perfectly what we already know and see in an obscure way. A director may not tell us anything we do not already know, but it is a great thing if he helps us to overcome our hesitations and strengthens our generosity in the Lord's service. However, in many cases, a director will reveal to us things which we have hitherto been unable to see, though they were staring us in the face. This, too, is certainly a great grace, for which we should be thankful.

One thing a good director will not do is make our ill-defined, unconscious velleities for perfection come true with a wave of the hand. He will not enable us to attain the things we "wish" for, because the spiritual life is not a matter of "wishing" for perfection. Too often people think that all they need to turn a "wish" into the "will of God" is to have it confirmed by a director. Unfortunately, this kind of alchemy does not work, and one who seeks to practice it is in for disappointment.

It often happens, as a matter of fact, that so called

"pious souls" take their "spiritual life" with a wrong kind of seriousness. We should certainly be serious in our search for God — nothing is more serious than that. But we ought not to be constantly observing our own efforts at progress and paying exaggerated attention to "our spiritual life." Some who lament the fact that they cannot find a director actually have all the opportunities for direction they really need, but they are not pleased with the available director because he does not flatter their self-esteem or cater to their illusions about themselves. In other words, they want a director who will confirm their hope of finding pleasure in themselves and in their virtues, rather than one who will strip them of their self-love and show them how to get free from preoccupation with themselves and their own petty concerns, to give themselves to God and to the Church.

This does not mean that all that passes for spiritual direction is really adequate. On the contrary, very often the "direction" given after confession is nothing more than a short, impersonal homily delivered to each penitent individually. It may be doctrinally correct, and perfectly good as a sermon. But direction is, by its very nature, something *personal*. It is quite obvious that a sister who knows she is receiving exactly the same vague, general exhortation as the twenty who went before her to confession hardly feels that she is receiving spiritual direction. Of course she is not.

Even then, she should try to make the best of it. If she

is humble enough to accept at least this, she will find that the Lord has His message for her in it all. And the message will be personal.

On the other hand, a priest who might be glad to give direction pertinent to the individual case is sometimes unable to do so because the penitent has not made a sufficiently clear manifestation of conscience.

4. *Manifestation of Conscience and Direction*

The manifestation of conscience, which is *absolutely necessary* for spiritual direction, is something apart from sacramental confession of sins. In actual fact, sometimes our real problems are not very closely connected with the sinful acts which we submit to the power of the keys. Or if they are connected, the mere confession of the sins does nothing to make the connection apparent.

Actually, sin usually presents itself to the confessor as something rather impersonal — genus and species are the same in everyone. In consequence, the best he can do is to respond with advice that is more or less general and universal. It may be good advice in itself and perfectly in accordance with moral theology, and yet not get anywhere near the real root of the concrete, personal problem in the soul of the penitent.

Those who have never stopped to make a distinction

between confession and direction may, when the time comes to have a director, fail to take advantage of the situation because they do not know how to make a manifestation of conscience. This is perhaps because they have a vaguely professional and technical idea of spiritual direction — the sort of thing we have outlined and perhaps caricatured in the first chapter. Direction for them is a strange, efficient, magical system. One comes to the director with complex ascetic problems and he resolves them with appropriate technical solutions. Hence the temptation to falsify the whole thing from the very start by coming in with an "interesting problem" or a "new case" — just to show how important and how different we are. This can sometimes happen. But usually we are so unimaginative that we simply cannot work up this kind of material, and we become discouraged. Naturally this is all very foolish.

If we are to take advantage of spiritual direction we must, on the one hand, avoid inertia and passivity — simply saying nothing and waiting for the "magic" director to read our minds and apply spiritual balm — and, on the other, we must not falsify and dramatize the situation by the creation of fictitious "problems."

What we need to do is bring the director into contact with our real self, as best we can, and not fear to let him see what is false in our false self. Now this right away implies a relaxed, humble attitude in which we *let go* of ourselves and renounce our unconscious efforts to maintain a façade. We must let the director know that

24

we really think, what we really feel, and what we really desire, even when these things are not altogether honorable. We must be quite frank about our motives insofar as we can be so. The mere effort to admit that we are not as unselfish or as zealous as we pretend to be is a great source of grace. Hence, we should approach direction in a spirit of humility and compunction, ready to manifest things of which we are not proud! This means that we must abandon all pugnacity about ourselves and get rid of our instinct for self-defence and self-justification, which is, in itself, the greatest obstacle to grace in our relations with a director.

The manifestation of conscience supposed by ordinary spiritual direction implies an atmosphere of unhurried leisure, a friendly, sincere and informal conversation, on a basis of personal intimacy.

The director is one who knows and sympathizes, who makes allowances, who understands circumstances, who is not in a hurry, who is patiently and humbly waiting for indications of God's action in the soul. He is concerned not just with this or that urgent problem, this or that sin, but with the whole life of the soul. He is not interested merely in our actions. He is much more interested in the basic attitudes of our soul, our inmost aspirations, our way of meeting difficulties, our mode of responding to good and evil. In a word, the director is interested in our very self, in all its uniqueness, its pitiable misery and its breathtaking greatness. A true director can never get over the awe he feels in the presence of a person, an immortal soul, loved by Christ, washed in His most Precious Blood, and nourished by the sacrament of His Love. It is, in fact, this respect for the mystery of personality that makes a real director : this, together with common sense, the gift of prayer, patience, experience, and sympathy.

Of course, as St. Theresa points out, he ought to be a theologian. But no amount of theological study can give a man spiritual discernment if he lacks the sense of respect for souls in their uniqueness, which is a gift of humility and love.

Manifestation of conscience in the deep sense of the word is often very difficult. It may be even more difficult than the confession of sins. One feels an inexpressible shame and embarrassment in laying open the inmost depths of his soul, even when there is nothing there to be ashamed of.

As a matter of fact, it is often harder to manifest the good that is in us than the evil. But that is precisely the thing about direction. We have to be able to lay bare the secret aspirations which we cherish in our hearts because they are the dear refuge to which we can escape from reality. We must be able to lay them bare, knowing well enough that even in manifesting them we run the risk of seeing them in a different light — in which they lose their mystery and their magic. The director has to know what we really want, for only then will he know what we really are.

The trouble is that very often we ourselves do not know what we "really want." And this brings us to an important but very delicate subject: the attitude of religious and of Christians in general toward *the will of God.*

Too often a legalistic concept of the will of God leads to a hypocritical falsification of the interior life. Do we not often unconsciously take it for granted that God is a harsh lawgiver, without interest in the thoughts and desires of our own hearts, seeking only to impose upon us the arbitrary dictates of His own inscrutable, predetermined plans? And yet, as St. Paul has said, we are called to *collaborate* with God. "We are God's coadjutors" (1 Cor. 3:9). As sons of God, we are called to use our freedom *to help God create His likeness in our own souls.* And of course, we help Him also to build His kingdom in the world. In this work of collaboration we are not mere passive and mechanical instruments. Our freedom, our love, our spontaneous contribution to God's work is itself the choicest and most precious effect of His grace. To frustrate this active participation in the work of God is *to frustrate what is most dear to His will.*

This means concretely that in spiritual direction it will be very important to discover what holy and spiritual desires in the soul of the penitent really represent a possibility of *a special, spontaneous and personal gift which he alone can make to God.* If there is some gift which he alone can give, then almost certainly God asks that gift from him, and a holy, humble, and sincere desire may be one of the signs that God asks it!

But this is where a certain unconscious hypocrisy comes in. We are afraid to make this spontaneous gift, afraid of spontaneity itself because we have been so warped by the idea that everything spontaneous is "merely natural" and that for a work to be supernatural it has to go against the grain, it has to frustrate and disgust us. The truth is, of course, quite different. It is necessary for us to frustrate and overcome our sensual, selfish and exterior self, the compulsive and automatic self that is really incapable of true love. But when we do this we set free our interior, simple self, our godlike self, the image of God, "Christ in us," and we become able to love God with spiritual liberty and make Him, in all simplicity, the gift that He asks of us.

But when we fear spontaneity, we tend to mask our desires and to present them by denying them as it were. We feel that the director will automatically reject anything that we really desire. We believe that both God and the director are predisposed, in advance, against everything spontaneous. Hence, rather than simply manifest what we really feel, or really desire, we say something else that we imagine we are expected to feel, expected to desire, and we give the impression that we do not desire what we secretly desire. This, for all our good intentions, is plain hypocrisy. The consequences are really quite dangerous, because if this is our concept of the interior life, then we are saying, in effect, that God wills a façade. And we concentrate on building this façade in our own life and perhaps even in the lives of others. The result is the falsification of the whole religious life of our community.

No, we must be perfectly open and simple, without prejudices and without artificial theories about ourselves. We must learn to speak according to our own inner truth, as far as we can perceive it. We must learn to say what we really mean in the depths of our souls, not what we think we are expected to say, not what somebody else has just said. And we must be prepared to take responsibility for our desires, and accept the consequences. This is neither hard nor unnatural, since every man coming into the world is born with this simplicity. It is the simplicity of the child, which we all unfortunately lose before we have a chance to make good use of it.

Incidentally, this childlike simplicity has nothing to do with the artificially cultivated effrontery of the average teen-ager today. Cynicism is not a deep conviction with him (he has no deep convictions). It is only a pose which he adopts because he is insecure and is afraid to lose the approval of his group.

True simplicity implies love and trust — it does not expect to be derided and rejected, any more than it expects to be admired and praised. It simply hopes to be accepted on its own terms. This is the kind of atmosphere which a good director tries to produce : an atmosphere of confidence and friendliness in which the penitent can say anything that is on his mind with the assurance that it will be dealt with *frankly and honestly*. If in trying to be sincere the penitent simply poses, then he must be prepared to take the consequences. But anything he says that is genuine, that really comes from his heart, will be understood and accepted by a wise director. Such real, genuine aspirations of the heart are sometimes very important indications of the will of God for that soul — and sometimes they must be sacrificed.

This gives us a clue to what the director is really seeking to find out from us. He does not merely want to know our problems, our difficulties, our secrets. And that is why one should not think that a direction session that does not tackle a problem has not been a success. The director wants to know our inmost self, our *real* self. He wants to know us not as we are in the eyes of men, or even as we are in our own eyes, but as we are in the eyes of God. He wants to know the inmost truth of our vocation, the action of grace in our souls. His direction is, in reality, nothing more than a way of leading us to see and obey our real Director — the Holy Spirit, hidden in the depths of our soul. We must never forget that in reality we are not directed and taught by men, and that if we need human "direction" it is only because we cannot, without man's help, come into contact with that "unction (of the Spirit) which teaches us all things" (1 John 2:20).

In manifesting our inmost aspirations and trials, we should strive above all to be perfectly frank and clear. Direction will school us in being true to ourselves and true to the grace of God. *The discipline of sincerity and simplicity which a good director will discreetly impose, perhaps by indirect means, is one of the most vitally necessary things in the interior life of religious today.*

Sometimes it seems that the so called "interior life" is little more than a web of illusion, spun out of jargon and pious phrases which we have lifted from books and sermons and with which we conceal, rather than reveal, what is in us. How often the director, listening to seemingly admirable religious souls, is saddened and chilled by the sense that a smug, unconscious complacency, armed with the cliches of pious authors, stands before him fully prepared to resist every advance of humility and truth. His heart is contracted by a kind of hopelessness, a feeling that there is no way of breaking through and setting free the real person who remains buried and imprisoned under the false front that has been acquired, unfortunately, as a result of religious malformation.

Perhaps unwise direction is itself to blame for this spiritual "warping" of the person. Such souls are really unable to manifest what is in them, because they have blinded themselves completely to what is there and put something else in its place. Yet they are in perfect good faith, and in a sense they have a kind of peace, based on the rigid structure of artificiality which they have erected precisely as a bulwark against anxiety. Perhaps sometimes a little anxiety can be a good thing!

In any case, the director must be on his guard against the unconscious spiritual vanity which makes virtuous souls seek to shine, in a subtle way, in his eyes and capture his approval. Where there is good, he should certainly approve and encourage it, in all simplicity. Artificial humiliations are not necessary to keep the soul humble. But the simplicity of the director and perhaps a gentle sense of humor will be alert to detect anything that savors of a pious "act" on the part of the penitent. Nothing does so much harm in direction as the acceptance by the director of an unconscious pretense of perfection in place of the real thing.

There is perhaps no more difficult and delicate task for the director than the guidance of Christians called to a life of interior prayer. This is rendered all the more arduous by the fact that there is so much pious nonsense written, printed, and said, about "mystics," "victim souls" and other such categories. Direction is very important in the life of prayer, but at the present time the situation is such that a director who is not very simple and very wholesome can do great harm to someone who might be quite close to God in prayer. The whole trouble comes from the inordinate reflection upon self that is generated by the consciousness of "degrees of prayer" and steps on the ascent of the "mountain of love." Actually, when a person begins to take his prayer life overseriously and thinks of it as something requiring especially earnest direction, he tends to undermine it by reflection. He starts looking at himself, judging his reactions, and worse still, deciding whether or not to make them known to the director. This of course is fatal to genuine prayer, and even in the long run leads to the ruin of perfectly good contemplative vocations. It would seem that most of the pseudo-technical questions that seem to require consideration in direction are completely useless and should be forgotten. What possible good can be done for a monk by deciding whether or not his contemplation is "infused"? Even those who are still interested in the defunct argument, acquired vs. infused contemplation, agree that in practice it makes little difference in the direction of a person whose prayer is simple and contemplative in a general way. A contemplative is not one who takes his prayer seriously, but one who takes God seriously, who is famished for truth, who seeks to live in generous simplicity, in the spirit. An ardent and sincere humility is the best protection for his life of prayer. A director who can encourage simplicity and faith will find many genuine, simple contemplatives responding to his guidance, with little or no nonsense about ligature, prayer of quiet, prayer of full union and so on. The trouble is not that such things are unimportant or unreal, but rather that the verbiage that tends to surround them actually gets between the contemplative and reality, between the soul and God.

The most dangerous thing about this kind of reflexive self-consciousness in prayer is that the soul turns into an opaque mirror in which the contemplative looks no longer at God but at himself. Such technical folly, together with the worse folly of visions and locutions that are taken seriously without sufficient reason, ends by the sanctuary of the spirit becoming a kind of abomination of desolation in which the voice of God cannot be heard because on all sides the walls re-echo with clichés from "spiritual authors."

An artificial gruffness and the use of deliberate humiliations will do nothing to remedy this state of affairs, if the director himself, even secretly, adopts the same false standard of values and declares implicitly, by the very way in which he "humbles" his penitent, that these are great graces capable of turning anyone's head. This is just another way of making the same mistake. Neither the director nor the one directed should become obsessed with the problem of gifts and graces, but should concern themselves with God the Giver, not with His gifts. The important thing is the will of God and His love. The more objective one can be about this, the better. Graces and gifts are never going to turn the head of anyone who keeps his attention fixed on God, instead of on himself, and the more truly contemplative a state of prayer is, the more will it be obscure and transparent and unaware of itself.

What has been said about graces of prayer applies in

equal measure to trials and passive purifications. The important thing is to quietly reassure the soul that seems to be anxious and upset, to create a proper understanding of spiritual trials without overdramatizing the "night" of the soul. In reality, there is just as much danger of self-contemplation in trials as in consolations, provided that the trials themselves are not really severe. A lot of darkness in prayer that glorifies itself as "passive purification" is perhaps in large measure a matter of boredom due to confusion and fixation upon the subjective and accessory aspects of the spiritual life. Let the soul get back into full contact with reality and the dryness will probably clear up to a great extent. Unfortunately, the routine and spirituality encouraged in certain contemplative communities tend to invite frustration and to glorify every form of infantile moodiness as a spiritual night. The victims of this kind of system are encouraged in masochism and self-pity on the ground that this has something to do with "contemplation." Actually, this is an evasion of grace and a pure pretense of spirituality. In the long run, it leads to various forms of escape, for example useless and futile activities, unnecessary work projects, etc., which are dreamed up more or less deliberately to break the spell of obsession with self. But they do not accomplish their effect, producing only a different kind of anxiety and a new frustration. What is really required is a normal, realistic and completely simple grasp of what the contemplative life is, in all its simplicity, with its humble, spontaneous activities, its genuine, if rustic, satisfactions, and the legitimate diversion that can come from a variety of reading and a broadening of healthy human interests, not at all incompatible with a life of prayer.

It is certainly not necessary to break up an unhealthy fixation on experiences in prayer by going to the other extreme and launching the bewildered subject into a round of parties and secular diversions, as too many directors might be prone to do. We must be careful to seek a happy and balanced medium. This consists neither in the extreme of self-conscious asceticism or the opposite extreme of self-abandoned sociability and conviviality, but rather in the recovery of a simple and wholesome ordinary life, lived at a moderate and humanly agreeable tempo, with a few very humble satisfactions and joys of a more or less primitive character. Manual labor (especially outdoor work) plays a very important part in this readjustment, not purely as a penance but also as a way of relaxing and refreshing the mind.

In summary, one of the most important benefits a director can bring to the prayer life of his contemplative penitents is to help them reintegrate their whole existence, as far as possible, on a simple, natural and ordinary level on which they can be fully *human*. Then grace can work on them and make them fully sons of God.

5. *Special Problems*

Once we have opened the depths of our soul to him, the director penetrates our motives and sees, though "through a glass darkly," to what extent they correspond to the truth and grace of God. The value of a director lies in the clarity and simplicity of his discernment, in sound judgment, rather than in the exhortation he gives. For if his exhortation is based on a wrong judgment, then it is of little value. In fact it may do harm. This faculty of supernatural discernment is a grace; in fact, it is a charismatic gift, a grace of a high order, given especially by God for the sake of souls. And such charismata are by no means as rare as one might imagine. The Holy Spirit still works powerfully in His Church, though His power is more hidden than it was in the first centuries! Have we any reason to doubt it?

Sometimes the light of truth given to the director pierces, in spite of us, through our unconscious armor. He may say something that troubles us deeply. We may rebel at first. We may imagine that he has made a serious error and does not understand us. We argue that everything he says ought to bring us peace — and this new statement of his brings profound disturbance! We may be tempted to reject his decision and disregard his advice, even to leave him altogether.

At such a time we must be on our guard. We may be

resisting the light of God. We may be refusing to accept a grace which will transform our whole lives. We may be hesitating and turning back on the threshold of one of those "conversions" which lead to a whole new level of spirituality and to deeper intimacy with Christ. Let us be very careful when we are angry with our director. Let us see if we cannot accept what he has said, no matter how wrong it may seem. Let us at least try to go along with him and see what comes of it.

A little good will, a little faith and a humble prayer to God may enable us to do what seemed to be impossible, and we may be surprised to find that an almost miraculous change has suddenly come over our life. Even when the director himself was clumsy or high-handed, God may reward our humility and good will with great graces.

Of course, as we have indicated above, it is quite possible that we have a director who does not understand us. There is no such thing as a perfect director, and even the most enlightened and sensitive spiritual guide can fail to respond to the delicate resonances which reveal the true inner secret of one's character. There are people who simply do not "click." The situation may be serious enough for a change of director to be indicated. For instance, if a director simply refuses to listen to our sincere views and rejects all serious discussion of them, it may be a reason to change. However, do not be too hasty. Give the matter time and thought. Have you really sufficient reason for changing? Supposing he does not understand you thoroughly: supposing there is a kind of wall between you: can you say that even then he has not revealed to you many important things that no one else has yet told you? If that is the case, then God is using him as an instrument, and you should stay with your director, unless it is quite clear that another and more understanding director is available. In any case, a change of director should be made only with prudent consideration, and if possible after consultation with a wise friend, a competent superior, or an alternate confessor — for example at the time of annual retreat or of extraordinary confessions.

What is the value of direction by mail? It should not be overestimated. An occasional letter from some spiritual guide who knows you well, and is a good theologian or a deeply spiritual person — this may be of some value. But direction by mail is seriously handicapped by one important thing: the lack of direct personal contact. In oral spiritual direction, much is communicated without words, even in spite of words. The direct person-to-person relationship is something that cannot be adequately replaced. Christ Himself said, "Where two or three are gathered together in My Name, there am I in the midst of them." There is a special spiritual presence of Christ in direct personal conversation, which guarantees a deeper and more intimate expression of the whole truth.

Of course, letters from a really good director are perhaps better than direct contact with a bad one. But most good directors have very little time to write long letters. They have too many other things to do.

One must not imagine that one owes strict obedience to the spiritual director. A director is not a superior. Our relation to him is not that of a subject to a divinely constituted juridical authority. It is rather the relation of a friend to an advisor. Hence, the virtue to be exercised in direction is docility rather than obedience, and docility is a matter of prudence. Obedience is a matter of justice. To ignore the guidance of a director may be imprudent, but it is not a sin against justice or against the vow of obedience.

We might add that theologians today discourage any such thing as a private vow of obedience to the director. However, in the case of people with scruples, they must follow to the letter the instructions given by the director and not quibble over words; it will be, in practice, a kind of obedience. But in this case the scrupulous person is incapable of practicing prudence, and consequently he must obey the director. He is in the position of a child who has to obey his parents since he cannot yet trust his own prudence.

One final point. The director is not a psychoanalyst. He should stick to his divinely given mission, and avoid two great mistakes. First, he should not become an amateur in psychotherapy. He should not try to concern himself directly with unconscious drives and emotional problems. He should know enough about them to recognize their presence. He should have a deep respect for man's unconscious, instinctual nature. He should not make the mistake of giving a direction that reinforces unconscious and infantile authoritarian trends. At the same time he should not be too easy and too soothing, giving approval to every whim, no matter how unreasonable.

Secondly, he should realize that psychological problems are very real and that when they exist they are beyond the range of his competency. He should not be one of those who derides psychiatry on principle and pretends that all emotional problems can be solved by ascetic means. He should know when to refer someone to a psychiatrist for proper treatment. He should not try to "cure" a neurotic by bluffing him, or jollying him along, still less by jumping on him!

We have taken a brief glance at some of the advantages of spiritual direction and at some of its problems. Inevitably, such a treatment as this lacks perspective. It gives the impression that there is always a great deal going on between the director and the one being directed. It creates the idea that the director has to be always on his toes to avoid being deceived — as if every direction session turned into a battle between light and darkness.

This is by no means the case. Once the director and

his penitent get to know each other, the direction generally goes on peacefully and uneventfully from month to month and from year to year. Great problems seldom arise. Difficulties are few. When they come up, they are handled simply and peacefully, without much fuss. There may be rare moments of difficulty and stress, but they pass by. One is tempted to think that all this is too tame, too quiet, too safe. It almost looks as if direction were a waste of time, as if it amounted to nothing more than a friendly chat about the trivial events of the season.

However, if we are wise, we will realize that this is precisely the greatest value of direction. The life that is peaceful, almost commonplace in its simplicity, might perhaps be quite a different thing without these occasional friendly talks that bring tranquility and keep things going on their smooth course. How many vocations would be more secure if all religious could navigate in such calm, safe waters as these!

WHAT IS MEDITATION?

To meditate is to exercise the mind in serious reflection. This is the broadest possible sense of the word "meditation." The term in this sense is not confined to religious reflections, but it implies serious mental activity and a certain absorption or concentration which does not permit our faculties to wander off at random or to remain slack and undirected.

From the very start it must be made clear, however, that reflection here does not refer to a purely intellectual activity, and still less does it refer to mere reasoning. Reflection involves not only the mind but also the heart, and indeed our whole being. One who really meditates does not merely think, he also loves, and by his love — or at least by his sympathetic intuition into the reality upon which he reflects — he enters into that reality and knows it so to speak from within, by a kind of identification.

St. Thomas and St. Bernard of Clairvaux describe meditation (*consideratio*) as "the quest for truth." Nevertheless their "meditation" is something quite distinct from study, which is also a "quest for truth."

Meditation and study can, of course, be closely related. In fact, study is not spiritually fruitful unless it leads to some kind of meditation. By study we seek the truth in books or in some other source outside our own minds. In meditation we strive to absorb what we have already taken in. We consider the principles we have learned and we apply them to our own lives. Instead of simply storing up facts and ideas in our memory, we strive to do some original thinking of our own.

In study we can be content with an idea or a concept that is true. We can be content to know *about* truth. Meditation is for those who are not satisfied with a merely objective and conceptual knowledge *about* life, *about* God — *about* ultimate realities. They want to enter into an intimate contact with truth itself, with God. They want to experience the deepest realities of life by *living* them. Meditation is the means to that end.

And so, although the definition of meditation as a quest for truth (*inquisitio veritatis*) brings out the fact that meditation is above all a function of the intelligence, nevertheless it implies something more. St. Thomas and St. Bernard were speaking of a kind of meditation which is fundamentally religious, or at least philosophical, and which aims at bringing our whole being into communication with an ultimate reality beyond and above ourselves. This unitive and loving knowledge begins in meditation but it reaches its full development only in contemplative prayer.

44

This idea is very important. Strictly speaking, even religious meditation is primarily a matter of thought. But it does not end in thought. Meditative thought is simply the beginning of a process which leads to interior prayer and is normally supposed to culminate in contemplation and in affective communion with God. We can call this whole process (in which meditation leads to contemplation) by the name *mental prayer*. In actual practice, the word "meditation" is quite often used as if it meant exactly the same thing as "mental prayer." But if we look at the precise meaning of the word, we find that meditation is only a small part of the whole complex of interior activities which go to make up mental prayer. Meditation is the name given to the earlier part of the process, the part in which our heart and mind exercise themselves in a series of interior activities which prepare us for union with God.

When thought is without affective intention, when it begins and ends in the intelligence, it does not lead to prayer, to love or to communion. Therefore it does not fall into the proper pattern of mental prayer. Such thought is not really meditation. It is outside the sphere of religion and of prayer. It is therefore excluded from our consideration here. It has nothing to do with our subject. We need only remark that a person would be wasting his time if he thought reasoning alone could satisfy the need of his soul for spiritual meditation. Meditation is not merely a matter of "thinking things out," even if that leads to a good ethical resolution. Meditation is more than mere practical thinking.

The distinctive characteristic of religious meditation is that it is a search for truth which springs from love and which seeks to possess the truth not only by knowledge but also by love. It is, therefore, an intellectual activity which is inseparable from an intense consecration of spirit and application of the will. The presence of *love* in our meditation intensifies and clarifies our thought by giving it a deeply affective quality. Our meditation becomes charged with a loving appreciation of the *value* hidden in the supreme truth which the intelligence is seeking. This affective drive of the will, seeking the truth as the soul's highest good, raises the soul above the level of speculation and makes our quest for truth a prayer full of reverential love and adoration striving to pierce the dark cloud which stands between us and the throne of God. We beat against this cloud with supplication, we lament our poverty, our helplessness, we adore the mercy of God and His supreme perfections, we dedicate ourselves entirely to His worship.

Mental prayer is therefore something like a sky-rocket. Kindled by a spark of divine love, the soul streaks heavenward in an act of intelligence as clear and direct as the rocket's trail of fire. Grace has released all the deepest energies of our spirit and assists us to climb to new and unsuspected heights. Nevertheless, our own faculties soon reach their limit. The intelligence can climb no higher into the sky. There is a point where the mind bows down its fiery trajectory as if to acknowledge its limitations and proclaim the infinite supremacy of the unattainable God.

But it is here that our "meditation" reaches its climax. Love again takes the initiative and the rocket "explodes" in a burst of sacrificial praise. Thus love flings out a hundred burning stars, acts of all kinds, expressing everything that is best in man's spirit, and the soul spends itself in drifting fires that glorify the Name of God while they fall earthward and die away in the night wind!

That is why St. Albert the Great, the master who gave St. Thomas Aquinas his theological formation at Paris and Cologne, contrasts the contemplation of the philosopher and the contemplation of the saints:

The contemplation of philosophers seeks nothing but the perfection of the one contemplating and it goes no further than the intellect. But the contemplation of the saints is fired by the love of the one contemplated: that is, God. Therefore it does not terminate in an act of the intelligence but passes over into the will by love.

St. Thomas Aquinas, his disciple, remarks tersely that for this very reason the contemplative's knowledge of God is arrived at, on this earth, by the light of burning love: *per ardorem caritatis datur cognitio veritatis.* (Commentary on St. John's Gospel, Chapter 5.)

The contemplation of "philosophers," which is merely intellectual speculation on the divine nature as it is reflected in creatures, would be therefore like a sky-rocket that soared into the sky but never went off. The beauty of the rocket is in its "death," and the beauty of mental prayer and of mystical contemplation is in the soul's abandonment and total surrender of itself in an outburst of praise in which it spends itself entirely to bear witness to the transcendent goodness of the infinite God. The rest is silence.

Let us never forget that the fruitful silence in which words lose their power and concepts escape our grasp is perhaps the perfection of meditation. We need not fear and become restless when we are no longer able to "make acts." Rather we should rejoice and rest in the luminous darkness of faith. This "resting" is a higher way of prayer.

MEDITATION IN SCRIPTURE

We read in Genesis that Isaac went out into the field in the evening to meditate (Gen. 24:63). What was he meditating about? The patriarchs were men very close to God, men to whom He spoke familiarly. He was always close at hand in the lives of Noe, Abraham, Isaac, Jacob. When the Jews invoked the God of Abraham, Isaac and Jacob, they invoked Him whom their fathers *knew*, Him who had promised salvation to them through their fathers. Although man was expelled from paradise, a few chosen persons still enjoyed something of the intimacy with God which had belonged to the old days when Adam and Eve heard His voice as He walked in the Garden of Eden in the early evening.

One reason why the Law was given to Moses on Sinai was that the Chosen People were afraid to speak directly with God or have Him speak to them.

And all the people saw the voices and the flames, and the sound of the trumpet, and the mount smoking: and being terrified and struck with fear, they stood afar off, saying to Moses: Speak thou to us, and we will hear; let not the Lord speak to us, lest we die! (Exodus 20:18–19).

Meditation on the Law of the Lord was now a valid substitute for the intimate familiarity with God which had been the joy and light of the patriarchs. How could this be so if meditation on the Law did not lead to a union of minds and wills with God, if meditation did not bear fruit in a holy and supernatural conversation with God, sanctified by filial fear, and consecrated by reverence, obedience and self-sacrificing love? The reward of this meditation was the light of supernatural prudence, a wisdom which penetrated the meaning of the Law. This meditation on the Law meant that men not only externally fulfilled its prescriptions but understood their import, saw them in relation to God's purposes for man. This understanding brought man face to face with the power and mercy of God, reflected in His promises to the holy nation and in His designs for them. The fruit of understanding was indefectible moral strength, supernatural courage.

Take courage therefore, and be very valiant: that thou mayst observe and do all the law, which Moses my servant hath commanded thee: turn not from it to the right hand or to the left, that thou mayst understand all things which thou dost. Let not the book of his law depart from thy mouth: but thou shalt meditate on it day and night, that thou mayst observe and do all things that are written in it: then shalt thou direct thy way, and understand it (Josue 1:7, 8).

This meditation must accompany the reading and

recitation of the Law : its words make some sense when they are in our mouths, but they only make complete sense if they are at the same time fulfilled in our lives. Meditation on the Law means therefore not only thinking about the Law, studying the Law, but living it with a full, or relatively full, understanding of God's purpose in manifesting to us His will.

But what is this purpose ? We shall see that God's real intentions for man are contained not only in the Law of His justice but also and especially in the promise of His mercy. All God's love for us was already implicitly contained in His promises to Abraham. The "just man lives by faith" in those promises.

The psalms everywhere sing of this "meditation" on the Law of God. But above and beyond the Law, the psalmists are carried out of themselves by their experience of God's mercy, by their realization of His *fidelity to His promises: Misericordias Domini in aeternum cantabo*! The psalms meditate not only on the goodness and beauty of the Law of God, and on the happiness of a life set in order by that Law, but above all on a supreme and ecstatic happiness which is the pure gift of God's mercy to the poor, to the *Anawin* — to those who, because they have no human hope, greatness or support, are therefore shielded and loved with a special power and compassion on the part of God. Meditation on the psalms, inspired by love, is the key to the great mystery of the divine compassion.

Hence the psalmist often sees himself raised above the level at which one finds God only through the medium of an outward expression of His will. Often the psalms bring us close to God Himself, the merciful God, the God who has promised justice to the oppressed, mercy and salvation to His people. The meditation of which the psalms are constantly singing often rises to the level of a penetrating experience of God's everlasting mercies. Then the psalmist breaks out into praise; for this experience of God's mercy is above all an experience that He is the supreme and transcendent Reality, and that He, the Lord who is above all gods, loves those to whom He has manifested His love and their salvation.

The mercies of the Lord I will sing forever.
I will show forth thy truth from generation to generation.
For thou hast said: mercy shall be built up forever in the heavens:
thy truth shall be prepared in them (Ps. 88:1–3).

It is clear, then, that the way of meditation is the way to perfect happiness, because it leads to the knowledge of the living God, to an experience of who He really is!

Blessed is the man who hath not walked in the counsel of the ungodly, nor stood in the way of sinners, nor sat in the chair of pestilence.
But his will is in the law of the Lord, and on his law he shall meditate day and night.
And he shall be like a tree which is planted near the run-

ning waters, which shall bring forth its fruit in due
season. And his leaf shall not fall off: and all whatsoever
he shall do shall prosper.

Not so the wicked, not so: but like the dust, which the
wind driveth from the face of the earth.

Therefore the wicked shall not rise again in judgment:
nor sinners in the council of the just.

For the Lord knoweth the way of the just: and the way of
the wicked shall perish (Ps. 1).

Monks meditate on the psalms when they sing
them. But St. Benedict in his Rule provides for a time
when this meditation on the psalms is carried on outside of choir. The meditation can have various degrees.
For beginners it means simply learning them by heart.
For those further advanced it means the intelligent
penetration of their meaning.

However this penetration of the meaning of the
psalms was not just a matter of studying them with the
aid of a commentary. It was a question of "savoring"
and "absorbing" the meaning of the psalms in the
depths of one's own heart, repeating the words slowly,
thoughtfully, prayerfully in the deepest center of one's
being, so that the psalms gradually come to be as intimate and personal as one's own reflections and feelings.
Thus the psalms "form" the mind and the heart of the
monk according to the mind and heart of Christ. Even
the perfect monk does not abandon his *meditatio
psalmorum* as if it were a mere exercise for beginners.

Contemplatives keep these holy words, as did Mary,

pondering them in their hearts so that they re-live the deep experiences of the psalmist, and in so doing are touched by the finger of God, raised to contemplation, and penetrate deeply into the mystery of Christ, which overshadows the whole Old Testament like the luminous cloud on Thabor. Christ is everywhere in the psalms, the Law and the Prophets. To find Him in them is to experience their perfect fulfillment because we find Him who is the life and meaning of the psalms, living within ourselves.

Jesus gave His disciples the sacrifice and sacrament of the Eucharist. This tremendous gift, containing in itself all the wisdom of God in mystery, sums up in itself all the mighty works of God, and is the greatest of them all. In this sacrament we are intimately united to Him, and bless Him who has "visited His people." The mystery of God's merciful love is revealed in the pierced Heart of Christ, the *magnum pietatis sacramentum*.

Meditation on this mystery, is, in some sense, essential to the Eucharistic sacrifice since Jesus said, "Do this in memory of me." The Mass is a memorial of Christ's sacrifice, not in the sense of an exterior commemoration, but as a living and supremely efficacious re-presentation of that sacrifice, pouring out into our hearts the redemptive power of the Cross and the grace of the resurrection, which enables us to live in God. Our participation in the Eucharistic sacrifice and our entrance with burning hearts into the mystery of Christ assumes in our lives the place which belonged to "meditation of the Law" in the lives of the Old Testament saints.

Nevertheless, as the New Testament does not do away with the Old, neither do we cease to meditate on the Law of the Lord. But our meditation is now nourished by the *memoria Christi* — the consciousness, the awareness, the experience of Jesus hidden in the Old Testament which He has now fulfilled.

This is what meditation meant to St. Paul : the finding of ourselves in Christ, the penetration of the Scriptures by divinely enlightened love, the discovery of our divine adoption and the praise of His glory.

Let us meditate on the Scriptures, which, as St. Paul says, were all written to fill us with the knowledge of God's promises and the hope of their fulfillment. "For what things soever were written, were written for our learning : that through patience and the comfort of the scriptures, we might have hope" (Romans 15:4). Believing in what we meditate, we are sealed, transformed, consecrated : "Signed with the Holy Spirit of promise." And to what purpose ?

That the God of our Lord Jesus Christ, the Father of glory, may give unto you the spirit of wisdom and of revelation, in the knowledge of him : the eyes of your heart enlightened, that you may know what the hope is of his calling, and what are the riches of the glory of his inheritance in the saints. And what is the exceeding greatness of his power towards us, who believe according to the operation of the might of his power . . ." (Ephesians 1:17–19).

MEDITATION—ACTION
AND UNION

All comparisons are defective in some respect. Our image of the sky-rocket might perhaps mislead imaginative minds. Meditation does not have to be colorful or spectacular. The effectiveness of our mental prayer is not to be judged by the interior fireworks that go off inside us when we pray. On the contrary, although sometimes the fruit of a good meditation may be an ardent sensible love springing from vivid insights into the truth, these so-called "consolations of prayer" are not to be trusted without reserve or sought for their own sake alone. We should be deeply grateful when our prayer really brings us an increase of clear understanding and felt generosity and we should by no means despise the stimulation of sensible devotion when it helps us to do whatever we have to do, with greater humility, fidelity and courage.

Nevertheless, since the fruit of mental prayer is harvested in the depths of the soul, in the will and in the intelligence, and not on the level of emotion and instinctive reactions, it is quite possible that a meditation that is apparently "cold," because it is without feelings, may be most profitable. It can give us great strength and spiritualize our interior life, lifting it above the level of the senses and teaching us to guide ourselves by reason and the principles of faith.

Sometimes a potentially good meditation can even be spoiled by emotion. The spiritual effect of grace may be frustrated, the will may remain inert while the germinating idea is sterilized by sentimentality.

This is one of the points at which ignorance makes progress in mental prayer difficult or even impossible. Those who think that their meditation must always culminate in a burst of emotion fall into one of two errors. Either they find that their emotions run dry and that their prayer seems to be "without fruit." Therefore they conclude that they are wasting their time and give up their efforts, in order to satisfy their craving for sensations in some other way.

Or else they belong to the category of those whose emotions are inexhaustible. They can almost always weep at prayer. They can quite easily produce sentiments of fervor, with a little concentration and the right kind of effort, whenever they desire them. But this is a dangerous form of success. Emotional versatility is a help at the beginning of the interior life, but later on it may be an obstacle to progress. At the beginning, when our senses are easily attracted to created pleasures, our emotions will keep us from turning to God unless they themselves can be given some enjoyment and awareness of the value of prayer. Thus the taste for spiritual things has to start out with a humble and earthly beginning, in the senses and in feeling. But if our prayer always ends in sensible pleasure and interior consolation we will run the risk of resting in these things which are by no means the end of the journey.

There is always a danger of illuminism and false mysticism when those who are easily swayed by fancy and emotion take too seriously the vivid impulses they experience in prayer, and imagine that the voice of their own exalted feeling is really the voice of God.

The proper atmosphere of meditation is one of tranquillity and peace and balance. The mind should be able to give itself to simple and peaceful reflection. Intellectual brilliance is never required. The will should find itself directed toward the good and strengthened in its desire for union with God. It does not have to feel itself enkindled with raptures of ardent love. A good meditation may well be quite "dry" and "cold" and "dark." It may even be considerably disturbed by involuntary distractions. St. John of the Cross says somewhere that "The best fruit grows in land that is cold and dry." But this arid meditation nevertheless fills the soul with humility, peace, courage, and the determination to persevere in negotiating the obstacles to our spiritual progress. Our meditations may be habitually quite prosaic and even a little dull. That does not matter, if they succeed in bringing the depths of our intelligence and will into a direct focus upon the things of God, no matter how obscure our spiritual vision may happen to be.

A good meditation does not necessarily give us an absolutely clear perception of the spiritual truth that we are seeking. On the contrary, as we progress in the interior life our grasp of divine things, in mental prayer, tends to become somewhat indefinite because our minds find themselves in the presence of mysteries too vast for human comprehension. It is necessarily impossible for the human mind on this earth to have a clear, comprehensive perception of the things of God as they really are in themselves. The contemplative "experience" of divine things is achieved in the darkness of "pure faith," in a certitude that does not waver, though it cannot grasp any clear human evidence for its support.

This cannot be understood unless we remember one absolutely fundamental truth : that the power of meditation is generated not by *reasoning* but by *faith*. It can be said, without fear of error, that our meditation is as good as our faith. Hence the aim we should keep in view, when we meditate, is not so much the penetration of divine truths with our intelligence, as the firm grasp of faith which enables us to embrace these truths with our entire being. This does not mean that intelligence is excluded from mental prayer, and replaced by a kind of pietistic obscurantism. For faith is after all an act of the intelligence, as well as of the will, elevated to a supernatural level by the light of divine grace. Everyone who meditates should realize the full import of St. Anselm's dictum: *credo ut intelligam*, "I believe in order that I may understand." Only firm faith can bring any real spiritual light to our life of prayer. In order to practice this faith, we need to concentrate upon certain sayings of Christ Our Lord in the Gospel, or other words of the divinely inspired Scriptures, and re-affirm our faith and our conviction that these are, in all truth, the words of salvation, the treasure hidden in the field, for which we must sell everything else, abandon every other truth, in order that we may come to God. We should let these "words of salvation" sink deeply into our hearts and take full possession of them. It is precisely when our prayer is dry that we can most fruitfully exercise our faith in this manner. And remember that faith can at times require much struggle and effort. Above all if it is honest. For we may have to face great difficulties and human uncertainties, and face them with sincere minds. Faith is a risk and a challenge, and it is most pure when we have to pay for it with effort and spiritual sacrifice. Such effort and sacrifice have their place in meditation.

If our mental vision of God and of the way to God tends to lose its sharp outlines in the "cloud of unknowing," there should never be any real confusion as to the object we are seeking: union with God.

Mental prayer need not make us *see* the God we seek, but it should always confirm us in our determination to seek Him and no other. It may not always show us clearly the way to find Him ; but it should always leave us more and more convinced that there is nothing else worth finding. Therefore, although the object of our prayer may be hidden in darkness, meditation nevertheless makes it ever more and more clear that this object is the one goal of all our efforts. In this sense God and the way to God become more and more perfectly "defined" as we advance in mental prayer.

* * *

Writers on mental prayer often stress the fact that meditation should bear fruit in particular virtues and other immediate, practical results. And it is quite true that meditation has a practical purpose since it must enlighten our actions and make them all bear fruit in communion with God.

Meditation can therefore be considered in relation to two ends, one of which leads to the other. The immediate end of our mental prayer may be the understanding of some particular truth, the resolution to embrace a particular course of action, the solution of a spiritual problem, all of which prepare us for the reception of a very definite and particular grace necessary for the practical fulfillment of our daily duties.

But the ultimate end of all mental prayer is communion with God. Of course it is quite true that meditation disposes us for an immediate practical end on earth, with a view to our future union with God in heaven. But what I mean to emphasize here is that every meditation, every act of mental prayer, even if it may have some immediate practical purpose, should also bring us into direct communion with God. This is the true fruit of meditation. Every other immediate practical purpose is secondary and subordinate to this one principle and all important end.

Let me take an example. Suppose that I meditate upon the patience of our Lord Jesus Christ in His Passion. Suppose that I do so with an immediate practical end : to help myself practice patience in a difficult situation which confronts me. My interior vision will be concentrated upon the Redeemer who, without anger or contempt, without rancor or perturbation, silently and with supreme interior tranquillity accepted the gravest injustice and ingratitude, not to mention the most painful of physical and moral suffering. I will see that He was able to undergo all this with a pure and disinterested mercy for all men, including those who put Him to death.

I will also realize that in doing so He was not merely leaving me an example to admire from a distance. By virtue of my baptismal vows I am *obliged* to follow that example and to reproduce in myself something of His patience, meekness and tranquillity under suffering. Jesus Himself said, "He who does not take up his cross and come after me cannot be my disciple" (Luke 14:27).

Therefore, with all this before my mind, I will begin to desire with all the power of my will to practice this same patience according to my capacity in my own trials. Knowing at the same time the weakness and imperfection of my own soul fettered by attachments, I will above all pray earnestly and humbly for the grace without which I can never hope to conquer my impatience, irritability, aggressiveness and self-righteous impulses to judge and punish other men.

Such a meditation is directly ordered to an immediate practical end. It is aimed at the practice of patience. It seeks the grace that will make me strong enough to be meek. Meekness and non-violent resistance to evil both require the highest kind of fortitude, a fortitude which can come to me only from the cross of Christ!

If well made, my meditation will bear fruit in an increase of fortitude in patience. My patience will help me to endure trials in such a way that my soul will be purified of many imperfections and obstacles to grace. I will learn to know better the sources of anger in myself. I will then grow in charity, and since charity is the source of supernatural merit, I will merit a higher degree of union with God in heaven.

Also, of course, I will be a more charitable and virtuous person here on earth. But that alone is not what I mean by the ultimate end of meditation. The ultimate end of meditation should be a more intimate communion with God not only in the future *but also here and now*.

Therefore, in order to make a really deep and mature meditation on the Passion of Christ, I must become *spiritually identified* with Christ in His Passion. This recalls what has been said above about our union with Christ in the Mass and especially at Holy Communion. The words of Pius XII concerning the liturgy might equally well be applied to Christian meditation; its function is to "reproduce in our hearts the likeness of the divine Redeemer through the mystery of the Cross."

Not that we must never meditate on any other mystery than the Passion; but since all grace flows from the pierced side of Christ on the Cross, the Passion of Christ is in fact the meritorious and efficient principle of our union with God and of our supernatural transformation. This is clear in the second chapter of St. Paul's Epistle to the Ephesians in which the Apostle declares that Christ on the Cross restored peace between man and man as well as between mankind and God. Christ has in fact taken all our enmities and "killed them in Himself upon the Cross," so that He is our "peace" and in Him we are all united, in one Spirit, with God the Father (Ephesians 2:11–22). Clearly the Cross and Resurrection of Christ are the very center of Christian mysticism.

This great theological truth makes it unnecessary to

inquire, at great length, in what our "communion" or "identification" with Jesus in mental prayer must consist.

This communion is not merely a psychological identification, a matter of emotional sympathy in which we stir up in our hearts what we imagine to have been the sentiments of the Redeemer on the Cross. Nor is this communion simply a moral one, in which we strive by our mind and will to produce in ourselves His ethical dispositions. Our identification with Jesus is spiritual and should, in many cases, also be sacramental or quasi-sacramental.

I mean by this that it is a union or identification in the order of grace or love. Grace comes to us above all by the use of prayer, the sacramentals and the sacraments. I have adopted the term "quasi-sacramental" to cover situations in which our mental prayer prolongs and develops our fruitful reception of the sacraments or in which, for instance, we meditate with the help of such sacramentals as the Bible, the Way of the Cross, or the rosary.

Grace is the principle of supernatural and spiritual life. It makes us sons of God. That is to say, it makes us live spiritually by the divine life itself. Nor is this divine life in our souls merely a figure of speech. Life expresses itself in vital activities. The supernatural life of grace not only vivifies the whole organism of the Mystical Body of Christ but also produces, in each of its living members, the activities of virtue and the life of contemplation which are the manifestation of God's special presence in the soul.

Now this life of grace is the life of Christ, the true Son of God. We share God's life through the merits of the Passion of Christ. By participating mystically in His Passion and death we become sons of God by adoption as He is the Son of God by nature. Our adoptive sonship is immersed, as it were, in the divine life which Jesus possesses by His own right as the Second Person of the Blessed Trinity. St. Thomas holds that Christ, as the "Head" of the Mystical Body, has the power to pour out grace into all the members of that Body, and this is not merely a theologian's opinion. The Church teaches us that in actual fact Jesus constantly sends forth the life-giving streams of grace into the souls of all those who are united to Him.

This very brief outline is sufficient to enable anyone to understand the one big principle upon which our identification with Christ in contemplative prayer must depend. Here is the principle. All the members of the Mystical Body of Christ have, in actual fact, the divine life of Christ within them and are "mystically" identified with Him in a broad sense of the word. This identification is effected by the reception of baptism or by any act of faith or contrition vivified by perfect charity. The identification is real, and it is in fact our supernatural life. However, *we are not conscious of it*. The identification which we seek to effect in mental prayer is therefore *a conscious realization of the union that is already truly effected between our souls and God by grace.*

This is the secret of mental prayer, as it is also the secret of contemplation. Unless our mental prayer does something to awaken in us a consciousness of our union with God, of our complete dependence upon Him for all our vital acts in the spiritual life, and of His constant loving presence in the depths of our souls, it has not achieved the full effect for which it is intended.

Contemplative souls generally have a special attraction to the presence of God within them, or to some other form of consciousness of God's nearness to their intimate being. This is a grace which, though quite normal in the spiritual life, is not shared by all. But even those who do not have this particular attraction ought to realize that the function of their mental prayer is to bring them somehow into conscious communion with the God who is the source of their natural and supernatural life and the principle of all the good that is in them.

HOW TO MEDITATE

Meditation is really very simple and there is not much need of elaborate techniques to teach us how to go about it. But that does not mean that mental prayer can be practiced without constant and strict interior discipline. This is especially true in our own time when the intellectual and moral flabbiness of a materialistic society has robbed man's nature of its spiritual energy and tone. Nevertheless, the necessity for discipline does not imply the obligation for all men to follow one identical and rigid system. There is a difference between being strict and being rigid. The well-disciplined soul, like a well-disciplined body, is agile, supple and adaptable. A soul that is not pliable and free is incapable of progress in the ways of prayer. An unwise rigidity may seem to produce results at first, but it only ends by paralyzing the interior life.

There are however certain universal requirements for the sane practice of mental prayer. They cannot be neglected.

Recollection

In order to meditate, I have to withdraw my mind from all that prevents me from attending to God present in my heart. This is impossible unless I recollect my senses. But it is almost useless to try to recollect myself at the moment of prayer if I have allowed my senses and imagination to run wild all the rest of the day. Consequently the desire to practice meditation implies the effort to preserve moderate recollection throughout the day. It means living in an atmosphere of faith and with occasional moments of prayer and attention to God. The world in which we live today presents a tantalizing problem to anyone who wants to acquire habits of recollection.

The price of true recollection is a firm resolve to take no wilful interest in anything that is not useful or necessary to our interior life. The world we live in assails us on every side with useless appeals to emotion and to sense appetite. Radios, newspapers, movies, television, billboards, neon-signs surround us with a perpetual incitement to pour out our money and our vital energies in futile transitory satisfactions. The more we buy the more they urge us to buy. But the more they advertise the less we get. And yet, the more they advertise the more we buy. Eventually all will consist in the noise that is made and there will be no satisfaction left in the world except that of vain hopes and anticipations that can never be fulfilled.

I say this in order to show that very much of what we read in magazines or newspapers or see and hear in movies or elsewhere, is completely useless from every point of view. The first thing I must do if I want to practice meditation is to *develop a strong resistance to the futile appeals which modern society makes to my five senses*. Hence I will have to mortify my desires.

I do not speak here of extraordinary ascetic practices; merely of self-denial required to live by the standards of reason and of the Gospels. In present-day America, such self-denial is apt to require heroism. In practice it may mean giving up many or most of the luxuries which I have come to regard as necessities, at least until I have acquired sufficient self-control to use these things without being enslaved by them.

The Sense of Indigence

In order to make a serious and fruitful meditation we must enter into our prayer with a real sense of our need for these fruits. It is not enough to apply our minds to spiritual things in the same way as we might observe some natural phenomenon, or conduct a scientific experiment. In mental prayer we enter a realm of which we are no longer the masters and we propose to ourselves the consideration of truths which exceed our natural comprehension and which, nevertheless, contain the secret of our destiny. We seek to enter more deeply into the life of God. But God is infinitely above us, although He is within us and is the principle of our being. The grace of close union with Him, although it is something we can obtain by prayer and good works, remains nevertheless His gift to us.

One who begs an alms must adopt a different attitude from one who demands what is due to him by his own right. A meditation that is no more than a dispassionate study of spiritual truths indicates no desire, on our part, to share more fully in the spiritual benefits which are the fruit of prayer. We have to enter into our meditation with a realization of our spiritual poverty, our complete lack of the things we seek, and of our abject nothingness in the sight of the infinite God.

The Prodigal Son in the parable can serve as our model. Having wasted his patrimony in a distant country, he was starving to death, unable even to get his hands on a few of the husks which were thrown to the swine he tended. But he "entered into himself." He meditated on his condition. His meditation was brief and to the point. He said to himself: "Here I am dying of hunger, while at home in my father's house the servants have plenty to eat. I will return to my own country and to my father and say to him: Father, I have sinned against heaven and against you, and I am no longer worthy to be called your son. Will you take me in as one of your hired servants?"

The Fathers of the Church saw that every one of us is more or less like the Prodigal, starving in a distant land, far from our Father's House. This is the common condition of mankind exiled from God and from Paradise by an inordinate preoccupation with perishing things and by a constant inclination to self-gratification and sin. Since this is in fact our position, and since our mental prayer is a journey from time into eternity, from the world to God, it follows that we cannot make a good meditation unless we realize, at least implicitly, the starting point of our journey.

This is true in one way or another on every level of the spiritual life. The saints are, as a matter of fact, much more keenly aware of the gulf between themselves and God than are those who live always on the periphery of sin. As we advance in the interior life it generally becomes less and less necessary for us to stir up in ourselves this feeling of exile and of spiritual need. The soul that is only dimly enlightened by God has very little conception of its own indigence. The most serious faults seem to it to be quite harmless.

Habitual self-complacency is almost always a sign of spiritual stagnation. The complacent no longer feel in themselves any real indigence, any urgent need for God. Their meditations are comfortable, reassuring and inconclusive. Their mental prayer quickly degenerates into day-dreaming, distractions or plain undisguised sleep. For this reason trials and temptations can prove to be a real blessing in the life of prayer, simply because they force us to pray. It is when we begin to find out our need for God that we first learn how to make a real meditation.

The Proper Atmosphere of Prayer

One who has reached a certain proficiency in the interior life can normally practice some form of mental prayer anywhere and under almost any conditions. But beginners and proficients alike need to devote some part of the day to formal meditation. This means choosing a time and place propitious for mental prayer, and the exclusion of all possible obstacles to meditation. It should not be necessary to remark that we can best meditate in silence and retirement — in a chapel, in a garden, a room, a cloister, a forest, a monastic cell.

Religious communities have a set time for the practice of mental prayer. Sometimes the meditation degenerates into a dreary routine of "points" read from a pious book followed by intervals of silence and communal wool-gathering. Discouraging as this procedure may sometimes be, there is nothing in it that makes a good meditation essentially impossible. The very superficiality of the "points" may well awaken in us an acute sense of spiritual indigence and make us seek the living God with deep anguish and humility!

The trouble is however that human nature yields easily to exasperation under the pressure of mechanical routine. Exasperation foments interior rebellion, which is an obstacle to good mental prayer. Nevertheless there will always be docile and humble spirits who will quietly recollect themselves and listen to the "points" and receive with deep gratitude the slightest suggestion they may offer. Such souls are capable of progress in spite of the apparent mediocrity of their environment.

Nevertheless, passive acceptance of mediocrity is an obstacle to progress in prayer. The chief trouble with pre-digested meditations imposed mechanically upon a whole group is that they tend to bring meditation into disrepute — especially in seminaries where the victims of this system do not hesitate to detect the faintest shadow of stupidity or artificiality and make it the subject of frivolous comment.

The religious orders have their mental prayer in common but systematization and routine are usually foreign to their spirit. Communal mental prayer presents no unusual problems in a contemplative monastery, provided the rule is kept and the proper conditions of silence and good order are maintained.

Everyone should try to set aside some part of the day in which he can pray under conditions which seem to be most favorable for himself. This does not mean that we should try to gratify ourselves even in spiritual things, but it is legitimate and even in some cases necessary for us to seek an atmosphere that really helps us to pray. Anyone who seriously wants to meditate should be allowed reasonable liberties in this regard.

Naturally speaking, the best position for meditation is a seated one. The sitting position is favored by a certain type of contemplative, and a quotation from that charming fourteenth-century mystic, Richard Rolle, may be adduced in witness to the fact: He says (in the *Form of Perfect Living*)

I have loved for to sit: for no penance, nor fantasy, nor that I wished men to talk of me, nor for no such thing: but only because I knew that I loved God more and longer lasted within the comfort of love than going, or standing, or kneeling. For sitting I am most at rest, and my heart most upward. But therefore peradventure it is not best that another should sit, as I did and will do to my death, save he were disposed in soul as I was.

Religious custom makes it easy for Catholics to meditate on their knees. It is usually better to remain quiet, to be still. But there is no reason why one should not also meditate walking up and down in a garden. In short, there is an almost infinite variety of places and positions that can be adopted in mental prayer. They are all accidental. The most important thing is to seek silence, tranquillity, recollection and peace.

The only thing that remains to be added, before we pass on, is a reminder of the importance of leisure in the life of prayer. Leisure is so poorly understood by some religious people that it is regarded as almost synonymous with idleness. Without making any distinction between fruitful and sterile leisure, these busybodies condemn all desire for leisure as a sin. They believe that a man who is not always on the move is wasting precious time. They do not realize the meaning of St. Thomas's definition of laziness. Laziness, says the Angelic Doctor, is a weariness of and distaste *for what is good*. He does not say that laziness is distaste for work, because he is careful not to identify work, as such, with what is simply "good." Yet it is true that our fallen nature needs to labor and suffer in order to arrive at its highest good, spiritual good. It follows that in most cases our laziness is, in fact, a distaste for the labor that is required if we are to procure this good for ourselves. Nevertheless, the fact remains that the highest spiritual good is an action which is so perfect that it is absolutely free of all labor, and is therefore at the same time perfect action and perfect rest. And this is the contemplation of God.

Now the Fathers of the Church well understood the importance of a certain "holy leisure" — *otium sanctum*. We cannot give ourselves to spiritual things if we are always swept off our feet by a multitude of external activities. Business is not the supreme virtue, and sanctity is not measured by the amount of work we accomplish. Perfection is found in the purity of our love for God, and this pure love is a delicate plant that grows best where there is plenty of time for it to mature.

This truth rests on an obvious natural foundation. Someone has said, "It takes time to be a genius." Many promising artists have been ruined by a premature success which drove them to overwork themselves in order to make money and renew again and again the image of themselves they have created in the public mind. An artist who is wise thinks more than he paints and a poet who respects his art burns more than he publishes. So too, in the interior life, we cannot hope to pray well unless we allow ourselves intervals of silent transition between work and formal prayer. In trying to turn out too much work for God we may well end up by doing nothing for Him at all and losing our interior life at the same time. St. Therese of Lisieux wisely reminds us that "God has no need of our works: He has need of our love."

The ideal of the contemplative life is not, however, the exclusion of all work. On the contrary, total inactivity would stultify the interior life just as much as too much activity. The true contemplative is one who has discovered the art of finding leisure even in the midst of his work, by working with such a spirit of detachment and recollection that even his work is a prayer. For such a one the whole day long is *otium sanctum*. His prayer, his reading, his labor all alike give him recreation and rest. One balances the other. Prayer makes it easy to work, work helps him to return with a mind refreshed for prayer. These conditions are well fulfilled in the sane, quiet round of St. Benedict's monastic day of liturgy, meditative reading and manual work in the fields.

Sincerity

Mental prayer is by its nature personal and individual. In common vocal prayer, and in the liturgy, it is understood that the words we utter with our lips may not necessarily express the spontaneous feelings of our heart at the moment. When we unite with others in liturgical prayer, we put aside our sentiments of the moment in order to unite with the thoughts and desires of the community, expressed in the liturgical prayers. These then become our own sentiments and raise us above our individual level, to the level of the mystical Christ, praying in the liturgy.

In mental prayer, it is still the mystical Christ who prays in us, but in a different way. The private prayer of an individual is still in some sense a prayer of the Church, but it has no official and public character. Yet it is the prayer of the Holy Spirit in a member of Christ, in one who is by his baptism "another Christ." The desires and sorrows of our heart in prayer rise to the heavenly Father as the desires and sorrows of His Son, by virtue of the Holy Spirit who teaches us to pray, and who, though we do not always know how to pray as we ought, prays in us, and cries out to the Father in us.

For you have not received the spirit of bondage again in fear; but you have received the spirit of adoption of sons, whereby we cry Abba, (Father). For the Spirit Himself giveth testimony to our spirit that we are the sons of God. And if sons, heirs also; heirs indeed of God and joint heirs with Christ: yet so, if we suffer with Him, that we may be glorified with Him. . . .

Likewise the Spirit also helpeth our infirmity. For we know not what we should pray for as we ought; but the Spirit Himself asketh for us with unspeakable groanings. And He that searcheth the hearts knoweth what the Spirit desireth; because He asketh for the saints according to God.

(Romans 8:15–17, 26, 27.)

It can therefore be said that the aim of mental prayer is to awaken the Holy Spirit within us, and to bring our hearts into harmony with His voice, so that we allow the Holy Spirit to speak and pray within us, and lend Him our voices and our affections that we may become, as far as possible, conscious of His prayer in our hearts.

This implies a difficult and constant attention to the sincerity of our own hearts. We should never say anything in mental prayer that we do not really mean, or at least sincerely desire to mean. One of the reasons why our mental prayer easily grows cold and indifferent is that we begin with aspirations that we do not feel or cannot really mean at the moment. For instance, we fall on our knees out of habit, and without directing our attention to God we begin to tell Him that we love

Him, in a more or less exterior and mechanical fashion, hardly even aware of what we are saying. It is true, that we have a more or less habitual desire to love God, and if we attend to what we are doing we are capable of "purifying our intention" more or less as if we were using a mental windshield-wiper, wiping away juridical specks of self-love. We don't really *want* things that go contrary to God and to His will.

Nevertheless, is it quite sincere for us to express deep sentiments of love which we do not feel? Especially if in actual fact our hearts are quite cold and our minds are pretty much taken up with distractions which, though we do not formally will them, are nevertheless in almost complete possession of our hearts at the moment?

Here sincerity excludes spiritual laziness. At such a time, the sincere thing to do is to regret one's distracted state, and to make an honest effort to pray while admitting that really one has begun without any desire to pray and has just started out of routine.

Sincerity demands that we do what we can to break the grip of routine on our souls, even if it means being a little unconventional. If we really do not feel like praying, it seems at least more honest to recognize that fact before God than to assure Him that we are burning up with fervor. If we admit the truth, we will start out on a basis of humility, recognize the need for effort, and perhaps we will be rewarded with a little of the grace of compunction, which is the most precious of all helps in mental or any other kind of prayer.

Compunction is simply an awareness of our indigence and coldness and of our need for God. It implies faith, sorrow, humility and above all hope in the mercy of God. For the man without compunction, prayer is a cold formality in which he remains centered on himself. For the man who has a sense of compunction, prayer is a living act which brings him face to face with God in an I-Thou relationship which is not imaginary but real, spiritual and personal; and the basis of this reality is our sense of our need for God, united with faith in His love for us.

If we compare the sobriety of the liturgy with the rather effusive emotionalism of books of piety which are supposed to help Christians to "meditate," we can see at once that liturgical prayer makes sincerity much easier. The liturgy takes man as he is: a sinner who seeks the mercy of God. The book of piety sometimes takes him as he is only on very rare occasions: on fire with exalted and heroic love, ready to lay down his life in martyrdom, or on the point of feeling his heart pierced by the javelin of mystical love. Most of us, unfortunately, are not ready to lay down our lives in martyrdom most days at six o'clock in the morning or whenever our mental prayer may occur, and most of us have little or nothing to do with javelins of mystical love.

Mental prayer should be affective, it should be a work of love. But it should not be operatic, or a work of spiritual melodrama. The super-affective quality of some pious literature is a remnant of the baroque piety and mysticism of past centuries — a piety and mysticism peculiar to Italy, France and Spain in the 17th and 18th centuries. This particular form of piety was, perhaps, a result of the vulgarization of the spirituality of several great modern saints who exercised a decisive influence on Catholic piety during the period.

One should be able to rise above mere fashions in piety, especially when these fashions wear themselves out. If we go back to the saints themselves, we find a much more pure, sober and virile spirituality than in their more superficial followers.

In reaction against the over-enthusiastic affectivity of such piety, there is perhaps a tendency, in modern America especially, to become colloquial and informal in the extreme. One chats amicably with "Jesus" and "Mary." Our Lady becomes "Mom." St. Joseph is "Dad." And we "just tell them all about ourselves, all day long." This can, in the long run, become even more artificial and obnoxious than the worst flights of baroque opera. Some people may feel as if this sort of thing is "spontaneous" because it happens to flow easily and without effort. But it may simply be a kind of pose they have picked up from what we might call the "comic book school of spirituality." It flourishes today in the popular religious press.

Concentration and Unity

We have already seen that progress in the life of prayer means the emergence of one dominant attraction — a concentration of the interior life on one objective, union with God. We have remarked that this objective is usually obscure to our experience. The desire for God becomes more intense and more continual, and at the same time our knowledge of Him, rising above precise and definite concepts, becomes "dark" and even confused. Hence the anguish of the mystic who seeks God in the night of pure faith, above the level of human ideas, knowing Him not by light but by darkness. Contemplative prayer apprehends God by love rather than by positive knowledge. But this union of love, which gives the soul an "experience" of God, is effected in the soul by the action of the Holy Spirit, not by the soul's own efforts.

At the beginning of the life of prayer it would be a manifest error to seek this simple and obscure unification of our faculties in God by simply abandoning all efforts to think, to reason, or to meditate discursively. Meditation is the normal path to contemplative prayer. We have to start out with certain simple concepts. Meditation makes use of definite theological and philosophical ideas of God. It deals with ideas and principles which, when the soul is enlightened by faith and moved to action by charity, bear fruit in deep supernatural convictions.

The success of meditative prayer depends on our ability to apply our faculties to these revealed truths collectively referred to as "The Word of God." Therefore, meditation must have a definite subject. In the beginning of the life of prayer, the more definite and concrete we are in our meditations the better off we will be. The discipline of concentrating on a particular, clear-cut subject tends to unify the faculties and thus to dispose them remotely for contemplative prayer.

The Subject of Meditation

The choice of a subject is obviously important in meditation. And it is immediately evident that since meditation is a personal and intimate form of spiritual activity, the choice should be personal. Most people do not meditate well on a "topic" imposed by someone else, especially if it is something abstract.

The normal subject of meditation, according to the Christian ascetic tradition, will be some mystery of the Christian faith. There is a difference between a mystery and a dogma. A dogma of the faith is a more abstract, authoritative statement of the truth to be believed, couched in its official formulation. Meditation on a dogma, in this technical sense, is bound to be a little cold and abstract, though there are minds that might thrive on it.

A mystery is not just the distilled and decanted formulation of a revealed truth, but that whole truth in all its concrete manifestation : in the mysteries of the faith we see God Himself, generally in one of those great theandric actions in which He has revealed Himself to us in a concrete and tangible form, has carried out the work of our redemption, communicated to us a share in His divine life and united us to Himself.

To meditate on a mystery of the faith in this sense means first of all to perceive it externally as it is presented to us, as part of the Church's experience. The Church's experience of the mysteries, if such a phrase may be permitted, is handed down from age to age in tradition. Tradition is the *renewal,* in each Christian generation and society, of the experiential knowledge of the mysteries of the faith. Each new age of Christendom renews its faith and its grasp of the mystery of salvation, the mystery of man united to God in Christ, and each age renews this fundamental experience of the Christian mystery in its own characteristic way.

To enter into the mysteries of the faith by meditation, guided by the spirit of the Church, especially by the spirit of the liturgy and of Christian art, is to renew in oneself the Church's experience of those mysteries by participating in them. And of course the full participation of the Christian in the mystery of Christ is sacramental, public, liturgical: in the sacraments and at Mass. Hence the close relationship between private meditation and the public worship of the Church.

Suppose we meditate on the Incarnation.

The obvious approach to this subject is first of all to *see* the mystery as the Church sees it: hence, we meditate on the Gospel of the Annunciation, or the Gospel account of the Nativity — especially in the liturgical context of the Masses for Christmas or of the Annunciation. Christian meditation on the Incarnation is nourished by the sacramental *experience* of this mystery, as it is lived and celebrated liturgically by the Church.

This "external" grasp of the mystery involves activity of the senses, the imagination, the emotions, the feelings, the affections. A Christian, by meditation and by participating in liturgical worship, comes to feel and act as if he had been present among the shepherds at Bethlehem. Bethlehem is part of his life. He is completely familiar with the Nativity as though it were an event in his own history. And indeed it is, though on a mystical and invisible level. The function of meditation is first of all then to enable us to *see* and *experience* the mysteries of the life of Christ as real and present factors in our own spiritual existence.

To make this experience deeper and more personal,

meditation seeks to read the *inner meaning* beneath the surface of the exterior, and also, (most important of all) to *relate the historical events given us in the Gospels with our own spiritual life here and now.*

In simple terms, the Nativity of Christ the Lord in Bethlehem is not just something that I make present by fantasy. Since He is the eternal Word of God before whom time is entirely and simultaneously present, the Child born at Bethlehem "sees" me here and now. That is to say, I "am" present to His mind "then." It follows that I can speak to Him as to one present not only in fantasy but in actual reality. This spiritual contact with the Lord is the real purpose of meditation.

From this simple example we see, once again, that the real function of meditation is to enable us to *realize* and to *actualize* in our own experience the fundamental truths of our faith.

But there are other subjects for meditation.

Our own life, our own experience, our own duties and difficulties, naturally enter into our meditations. Actually, a lot of "distractions" would vanish if we realized that we are not bound at all times to *ignore* the practical problems of our life when we are at prayer. On the contrary, sometimes these problems actually *ought to be* the subject of meditation. After all, we have to meditate on our vocation, on our response to God's will in our regard, on our charity towards other people, on our fidelity to grace. This enters into our meditations on Christ and His life; for He desires and intends to live in us. The Christ-life has, as its most important aspect for each of us, *His actual presence and activity in our own lives.*

Meditation that ignores this truth easily tends to be aimless and confused.

Hence we cannot help sometimes meditating on our own lives, on what we have done, on what has happened to us, on what we intend to do. But in the event that these things intrude upon our prayer unexpectedly, we should tie them in with our faith in Christ and in Divine Providence. We should try to see our lives in the light of His providential will for us and for mankind. And by the same token we must sometimes meditate on the events of the history of our time and try to penetrate their terrible significance.

I would be inclined to say that a nun who has meditated on the Passion of Christ but has not meditated on the extermination camps of Dachau and Auschwitz has not yet fully entered into the experience of Christianity in our time. For Dachau and Auschwitz are two terrible, indeed apocalyptic, presentations of the *reality* of the Passion renewed in our time. Many pious people might be inclined to think that such things were "distractions" and attempt to exclude them from their minds. If such a revulsion were elevated to a level of strict principle and unvarying policy, it would lead to a complete lack of realism in the spiritual life. Such things should be known, thought about, understood in prayer. Indeed, the contemplative above all should ruminate on these terrible realities which are so symptomatic, so important, so prophetic.

The only reservation to be made here is with regard to one's approach to these things. Obviously the newspapers or news magazines give only a superficial and generally slanted view of events, and a view so shallow and secularized that it cannot possibly lend itself to "meditation" or serious thought at all. One has to see these things with a little depth, and without partisan prejudice. Otherwise one's meditation will be nothing but a jumble of absurd political clichés and self-complacent rationalizations which will be worse than useless, and will of course really prove harmful to the inner life.

Let us not forget the importance of meditation in the life of a man like Gandhi, one of the few really outstanding spiritual figures who had a part to play in modern political life. With him, it was a religious and spiritual obligation to understand, by meditation, the inner significance of events and political pressures, not in order to gain power but in order to liberate and defend man, the image of God.

Fundamentals

In order to understand even the trivial events of our

own lives, we need to *create a religious perspective* in which to view everything that happens. This perspective demands first of all that we frequently renew the realization of the fact that we must die and that our life must pass through the inexorable light of judgment. One who never thinks of the hour of his death cannot make really spiritual decisions during his life. He will never be anything more than a short-sighted opportunist whose decisions will have no lasting value.

Above all, our life should always be seen in the light of the Cross. The Passion, Death and Resurrection of Christ the Lord have entirely changed the meaning and orientation of man's existence and of all that he does. One who cannot realize this will spend his life building a spider's web that has no substance and no real reason for existence.

A meditation that passes superficially over many topics ends by being no meditation at all. It only weakens and dissipates our faculties, leaving them slack and unprofitable. They have been incited to work, but no work has been done.

In order to learn to gather our faculties on one point it is well to begin meditating with the help of a book. I do not mean that one must necessarily use a book of formally prepared meditations. Any serious book about the things of God and the spiritual life can provide us with matter on which to concentrate our minds. But in order to focus our minds on any truth, we normally need the help of our senses. Therefore, at the beginning of the spiritual life, it is usually best to meditate on truths that present themselves under some concrete form, for instance in a parable or in some graphic saying or action of one of the saints, or of Christ our Lord.

All the ancient philosophies and all the higher forms of religious thought have made use of parables and simple imaginative figures to convey the deepest truths, and nowhere is this more true than in the Bible. Here God has revealed to us His mysteries with a graphic simplicity and concreteness which makes them accessible to every race and century. There is therefore no better book of meditations than the Bible, and especially the New Testament. *Lectio Divina,* or the meditative reading of Sacred Scripture, was considered by the Fathers of the Church to be the normal foundation for an interior life of meditation and prayer.

An even simpler and more helpful approach to meditation is to make a deep reflective reading of the liturgical texts from the Old and New Testaments as they are presented to us, for instance, Sunday by Sunday, in the Missal. In this way our meditations can be perfectly co-ordinated with the liturgical cycle. This has the advantage of bringing our minds and hearts into a more perfect union with the prayer of the whole Church and thus disposing us to receive in greater abundance the graces which God pours out upon the world in answer to that prayer.

Here it might be worthwhile to outline the simple essentials of meditative prayer, in schematic form.

1) *Preliminary*: a sincere effort of recollection, a realization of what you are about to do, and a prayer of petition for grace. If this beginning is well made, the rest ought to follow easily.

2) *Vision*: — the attempt to see, to focus, to grasp what you are meditating on. This implies an effort of *faith*. Keep working until faith is clear and firm in your heart (not merely in your head).

3) *Aspiration*: — From what you "see" there follow certain practical consequences. Desires, resolutions to act in accordance with one's faith, to live one's faith. Here, an effort of *hope* is required — one must believe in the *possibility* of these good acts, one must hope in the fulfilment of good desires, with the help of God. Above all, one must have a sincere hope in the possibility of divine union.

4) *Communion*: — here the prayer becomes simple and uncomplicated. The realization of faith is solid, hope is firm, one can rest in the presence of God. This is more a matter of simple repose and intuition, an embrace of simple *love*. But if activity is required, let love have an active character, in which case the prayer is more like the last level (3). Or love may take rather the form of *listening* to the Beloved. Or the form of *praise*. More often than not, we can be content to simply rest, and float peacefully with the deep current

of love, doing nothing of ourselves, but allowing the Holy Spirit to act in the secret depths of our souls. If the prayer becomes confused or weak, we can return to one of the earlier stages, and renew our vigilance, our faith, our love.

We can end with a brief and sincere prayer of thanksgiving.

TEMPERAMENT AND MENTAL PRAYER

The precise way in which each individual makes his meditation will depend in large measure upon his temperament and natural gifts. An intellectual and analytic mind will break down a text into its component parts, and follow the thought step by step, pausing in deep reflection upon each new idea, in order to examine it from different points of view and draw forth all its hidden implications, both speculative and practical.

But analysis must not go too far. The mind must ascend, by reasoning, to the threshold of intuition. Meditation enters into its full swing, for an intellectual, when his mind can grasp the whole content of the subject in one deep and penetrating gaze. Then he rests in this intuition, letting the truth sink in and become a part of himself. Above all, intuition, setting the intelligence temporarily at rest, should leave the will free to adapt itself to the practical consequences of the truth thus seen and to direct our whole life in accordance with it.

Such minds as these — which are a minority — can fruitfully meditate on an article of the *Summa Theologica* or on any other theological text. But even they cannot always be contented with an intellectual approach to supernatural things. For a theologian, in practice, mental prayer should become a kind of refuge from his speculative study, an oasis of affectivity to which he can retire to rest after his intellectual labor. In any case, the prayer of love is always higher than mere mental considerations. All mental prayer, whatever may be its beginnings, must terminate in love.

Other less speculative minds approach the truth with a more immediate intuition, apprehending it in its wholeness as beauty rather than as truth. The radiance that pours forth from a spiritual intuition of the real is a pure light that captivates the whole soul. Sensible beauty loses its grip on the mind that finds itself momentarily under the spell of that *splendor veritatis,* the radiance of truth, the "beauty ever ancient and ever new" which finally brought peace to the soul of St. Augustine.

The majority of men need to practice a way of meditation that is more firmly rooted in the senses. For these, concentration depends on a mental picture and an important element in their mental prayer will be the exercise which St. Ignatius Loyola calls "application of the senses." In other words, they must take a concrete religious subject — a scene from the Gospels — and try to make all its sensible elements vividly real to their imagination.

This imaginative realization of a religious subject has

a very definite practical purpose. It is supposed to pave the way for living spiritual contact with God. Meditating on the Gospels, we place ourselves, as far as we can, in the presence of Jesus. We arouse in our hearts the dispositions that we would hope to have if we were speaking with Him or listening to His words. We act interiorly just as if we were talking with our divine Redeemer. What Jesus said twenty centuries ago is also addressed to us now. He may not be physically present to me, here and now, as man, but He is present as God. His divinity, which is the center and source of my own being, is also the very Being of His Humanity. Consequently the Christ who lives and speaks in the Gospel is much more truly present to me than the persons around me with whom I speak and deal in my daily life.

It is therefore by no means a mere play of fancy to place ourselves in the presence of Christ in a scene from the New Testament. However, it must be remembered above all that the function of this technical device is to incite us to acts of the theological virtues of faith, hope and charity, which are the principles of Christ's supernatural presence in our souls.

The true end of Christian meditation is therefore practically the same as the end of liturgical prayer and the reception of the sacraments: a deeper union by grace and charity with the Incarnate Word who is the only Mediator between God and man, Jesus Christ.

The peculiar value of mental prayer however is that it is completely personal and favors a spiritual development along lines dictated by our own particular needs. The interior life demands of us a heroic struggle to practice virtue and to detach ourselves from inordinate love of temporal, created things. We cannot possibly bring our souls to renounce our most powerful natural desires unless we somehow have a real and conscious appreciation of our contact with something better. The love of God remains a cold and abstract thing unless we can bring ourselves to realize its deeply intimate and personal character. We can never hope, on earth, to achieve anything like a clear realization of what it means to be loved by the three divine Persons in one divine nature. But it is very easy to appreciate the love of God when we see it concretized in the human love of Jesus Christ for us. This is the best and most logical foundation for a life of faith and therefore this above all should be the primary object of meditation.

SUMMARY AND CONCLUSION

Meditation is spiritual work, sometimes difficult work. But it is a work of love and of desire. It is not something that can be practiced without effort, at least in the beginning. And the sincerity, humility and perseverance of our efforts will be proportionate to our desire. This desire in turn is a gift of grace. Anyone who imagines he can simply begin meditating without praying for the desire and the grace to do so, will soon give up. But the desire to meditate, and the grace to begin meditating, should be taken as an implicit promise of further graces. In meditation, as in anything else in the Christian life, everything depends on our correspondence with the grace of the Holy Spirit.

Meditation is almost all contained in this one idea: the idea of *awakening* our interior self and attuning ourselves inwardly to the Holy Spirit, so that we will be able to respond to His grace. In mental prayer, over the years, we must allow our interior perceptivity to be refined and purified. We must attune ourselves to unexpected movements of grace, which do not fit our own preconceived ideas of the spiritual life at all, and which in no way flatter our own ambitious aspirations.

We must be ready to cooperate not only with graces that console, but with graces that humiliate us. Not only with lights that exalt us, but with lights that blast our self-complacency. Much of our coldness and dryness in prayer may well be a kind of unconscious defence against grace. Without realizing it, we allow our nature to de-sensitize our souls so that we cannot perceive graces which we intuitively foresee may prove to be painful.

Meditation is then always to be associated in practice with abandonment to the will and action of God. It goes hand in hand with self-renunciation and with obedience to the Holy Spirit. Meditation that does not seek to bring our whole being into conformity with God's will must naturally remain sterile and abstract. But any sincere interior prayer that really seeks this one all important end — our conformity to God's will in our regard — cannot fail to be rewarded by grace. It will prove, without question, to be one of the most sanctifying forces in our lives. And St. Teresa of Avila believed that no one who was faithful to the practice of meditation could possibly lose his soul.